Why Whole? W.H.O.L.E. wa painful and disappointing dating experience and extreme exhaustion, burnout, idolatry, and anxiety as a result of workaholism. I was deeply depressed and suicidal because I wholeheartedly believed that God plus someone and something made me whole. It was not until I came to the end of myself that He opened my eyes and heart to the overwhelming peace, joy, and steadfast love that was there for me all along.

As a single woman and teacher, it is my aim to help women of all ages and backgrounds to find their fulfillment in the Lord and Him alone. My aim is to help teachers, schools, and fragile women and girls pursue Christ and His wholeness. I want people to know, experience, and live out the Gospel. This organization was established to provide resources, assistance, and encouragement to schools, teachers, churches, women, and girls.

"What Happens When A Black Girl Doesn't Feel Like Magic?" is a book that came from that painful experience. God wants us to run to Him when the sadness and pressures of life become overwhelming. He brings us the love, joy, and peace that we all long for.

What Happens When A Black Girl Doesn't Feel Like Magic? by Chaquana M. Muhammad Townsend

When a black girl doesn't feel like magic, she hides behind her successes and finds her significance in performance. She's smart enough to know that people only call you "magic" when you are performing and living up to their standard. She masks her discomfort and *pain with a "Never Let Them See You Struggle Mentality" because after all, her black is magic, right?*

Her magic comes with a hidden fight to believe God loves the sinner who was discarded and taken advantage of continuously. This black girl fights to believe that if Jesus saw her daily struggle to love, to stay pure, to show His love to others, He would hide His face in rejection. What if anxiety makes this black girl feel less magical? What if academic success and being the best only fuel the loss of "Black Girl Magic?"

What if we could reverse what "Black Girl Magic" really is? Could we add the pain and successes into the equation? What if my "Black Girl Magic" came with wounds and scars that still needed ointment from time to time? What if it came with beauty that was deeper than a degree or financial success? What if it came with truth, honesty, rawness, ratchetness, and excellence all at the same time? Would it still be magical?

"Black Girl Magic" is Harriet Tubman, Maya Angelou, Oprah Winfrey, the R&B Legend and Queen Mary J. Blige along with the countless women who have seen and overcome the highs and lows of this life! Women who have seen the struggle, yet they contain to soar! Pain and
beauty sit at their doorstep only to create more beauty because "Black Girl Magic" is the ability to get up even when you don't want to . It's the ability to keep fighting when life has knocked you out! It is freedom, victory, triumph, and persevering through the rain. We are "Black Girl Magic!"

Table of Contents

Acknowledgements

First, I want to acknowledge my Lord and Savior Jesus Christ. He is the very reason why I am here and why I am able to go on each and everyday. He is my healing balm, and my comforter in and through every trial. He is my ultimate King, lover, and ruler, and I am so grateful to be His. He has truly restored my innermost being! I will live for Him because He deserves it.

Second, I want to thank my friends, family, and church family for being there for me. I am grateful for every person who has encouraged me, prayed for me, and lived in a way that pointed me to Jesus. Thank you to my best friend Kellee for being my ride or die partner for life. Shout out to my mother, father, sister, brothers, and beautiful nieces and nephews. I love you guys!

Lastly, thank you to those who have supported me in dance, teaching, and writing this book. Thank you for encouraging me through the writing process. May God bless you all! This book would not be here without you. I am forever grateful!

Foreword

Keelan Adams, Associate Pastor of Flatline Church at Chisolm:

This work paints a beautiful picture of God's providence, redemption, sanctification, and a little girl who grows into a woman that looks back and sees God's sovereign hand of protection over her entire life. This is an "open book" of sorts into the deep chambers of the author's heart. Herein, women can learn lessons from the implications of each mistake and error. On the other hand, this work issues a clarion call for men to take note of biblical manhood with the stark contrast of manhood run amuck. Altogether, this book helps both men and women see their intrinsically depraved condition and throughout introduces them to the only Savior who is able to provide a remedy for such ailments. His name is Jesus!

Alonzo Brown, Associate Pastor of Strong Tower at Washington:

Chaquana is one of the most authentic and sensitive people I know! In this book, Chaquana does a good job taking you through the dark roads she has traveled and bringing the reader to come away with enormous hope! This easy read has a sad reality...her story is common amongst a lot of people. The difference with her experiences is though she's traveled down these dark, familiar roads many have traveled, another wonderful story unfolds from a purposeful and loving Father who is there giving power and most importantly, Himself. Chaquana's story says we are never alone, even in our darkest valleys because we have a Savior who understands exactly where we are through His own personal experiences. He turns our dark roads to highways of healing and light! Great job Quani!

LONGING TO BE LOVED/CHILDHOOD

One of my deepest desires and deepest flaw is the desire to be wanted and loved. I have learned a few things about myself over the years: I am loyal, deeply committed, and consistent even when I don't get the same thing in return. I desired these things growing up; however, I never got them from the people I valued the most. My story and upbringing are a clear sign and testament of a young girl starved for affection. I was born on October 15, 1988 in Bronx, New York. I was born to a crack addicted mother and an abusive father. My father's verbal abuse showed itself when I finally started a relationship with him in my teens, but my mother experienced his physical and mental abuse. I was three pounds and eleven ounces due to my mother's drug addiction. My sister Nikki and I were both born premature, yet we grew into healthy young women. My sister and I are eleven months apart. I also have two older brothers, David and Benjamin. We were born in the 80's, but the 90's era had a hold on us! We loved SWV, Mary J. Blige, Mariah Carey, Biggie Smalls, and the list goes on and on. Since we lived in both New York and New Orleans during our younger years, we were music heads and I was the natural dancer. Life in both places was fun, but it also brought on challenges that caused deep wounds and scars that still plague me today. I had beliefs and values as a believer that the Lord has completely changed and restored; nonetheless, I am still recovering even at 29 venturing into 30.

Growing up, my sister and I were inseparable. In other words, we were never apart, literally. We are like night and day. Csniqua is like fire, and Chaquana is like ice! I remember a teacher in high school pointing out the clear difference in our personalities. I was overly obedient and rarely got into trouble. My sister, on the other hand, was outspoken and fearless! She was the popular girl, and I was the nerd who hung out with Asians, Hispanics, and Blacks. I loved reading and writing because it was one of the places I felt the safest. My brothers lived with us as well; however, one of my brothers moved to New York to live with his father. My mother has four children, two girls and two boys. I am the youngest child. My world was turned upside down at a very young age. I was only four. One day, I got the bright idea to take a lighter and light a mattress just for fun. My grandmother came in the room to put out the flame with water, but it was too late. Her hand was burned slightly, and we lost our home. We moved into a shelter, and then we finally moved to New Orleans to be near my great uncle. My grandmother became our sole provider while my mother stayed in New York for several years.

New Orleans was the number one murder capital in 1992. We lived in the 9th ward, and it had its challenges. My grandmother did an amazing job at affirming her grandchildren in every way. I told her I wanted to be a doctor, and she called me her future doctor. She never talked down to us, and her encouragement helped me to excel in school. She slipped up once and called me stupid for my actions when I was being disobedient and immediately apologized. She was present with homework, school activities, and graduations, yet I was longing for the love of mother and father. Although she was my hero and an angel on earth, she couldn't heal the void of affirmation and acceptance that I craved from my parents.

It's funny how children cry out for love and acceptance in so many ways. I never felt pretty enough, small enough, or smart enough because I longed to hear it from my parents. I remember talking to my Dad once when I moved to New Orleans. When I was a little girl, I remember him buying sundresses for Nikki and me. I was so happy to receive and wear that dress. When it came to my mother, I remember having dreams, tantrums, and long bouts of crying because I just wanted a mother's love and touch.

My mom decided to come to New Orleans to stay for sometime, and it was okay. Although Nikki and I were happy she was there, we soon realized she didn't know how to parent us. We were very afraid of her because she didn't play with us; however, we knew in our hearts that our grandmother played the better role of a mother. She gave us so much love and care. We never went without anything! Christmas was my favorite time of the year because she made it so worth it! The presents that we desired were received, and we loved the whole idea of gifts! I never missed a meal, and I was cared for so tenderly. Nonetheless, I had a complex. I was overweight and filled with fear and shame due to sexual abuse.

I love the phrase, "Black Girl Magic"; however, that magic

never really resonated with me. From the time I was four all the way up to the present, I have always fought to believe I was worth loving. It's funny how one moment and multiple acts of sin committed against you, can cause you to think that something is inherently wrong with you. Now, I don't want to play the victim role because I am aware of the reality of being born a sinner. However, as a young girl with inconsistent parents and circumstances beyond my control, I learned to dance and become friends with shame. I was four or five when I first encountered a young man. I remember it like it happened the other day.

I was playing on the bed with a t-shirt and panties on, innocently rolling on the bed. A friend of my older brother looked at me and pointed towards my lower parts. He asked, "What's that?" I looked at him and smiled. I knew what he was saying, but I knew it was wrong. He asked could he touch me, and I said yes. In that moment, as a young girl, I felt wanted and taken advantage of at the same time. I liked the attention, but I hated what it cost me. I wish I could say it was the first and last time it happened, but I became numb to young men touching me and calling me beautiful. Everytime it happened, I never said stop. I let them have their way carrying the guilt and shame with me. I remember flirting with an older man at a birthday party after being molested the first time. My oldest brother walked into my room and stated loudly, "Quani, I heard you were acting like a hoe!" I was five at the time. I crawled under my bed and cried. That was the first time in my life that I vividly remember hating myself and wishing I could disappear. The self-hate began right after that.

I learned a core belief at a very young age: "You have something that men want." The sexual abuse caused me to want men and hate them at the same time. I didn't feel safe with them. My dad wasn't around until I turned 14. I would fantasize about having children minus the father being there because that was all I knew. Even as a young girl, I internalized giving women a try because I felt so unsure of man's ability to love me and stick around. What hurt the most about the abuse was a sad reality: I knew these men because they were friends of the family and one happened to be a cousin. During my elementary school years, I experimented with a girl amongst other things. I vividly remember watching a porn my brother had lying around. I remember humping objects and a girl in particular. I showed her my lower parts, and she showed me hers. I thought it was fun, but the enemy gave me a taste of the other side. It felt safer than a man, so we fooled around a couple of times. I still liked boys, but women caught my eye and attention too.

I can recall being head over heels over a guy named Justin, a friend of my brother. In my mind, he was the finest thing I had ever seen! He had beautiful caramel skin, and I could stare at him forever. My heart and stomach went crazy every time he was around. One day, I got the courage to write him a note. It said these alarming words: "I like you. Do you like me? Check yes or no." After he read the note, he ripped it up and threw it on the ground. My heart was crushed by this teenage boy who rightfully rejected a young girl in elementary school. The experience of molestation and neglectful parents left me insecure and longing for affirmation and love. I performed academically to show how worthy I was to be loved, but inwardly I felt like damaged goods and firmly believed I was rejected by my parents and abused by men because something was wrong with me.

NO VOICE

Believing you have "no voice" is a learned belief. It started with a moment, a comment, an unintentional act that altered the mind of a young Queen longing to fly. In every instance of my life, I believed my voice and opinion didn't **matter.** I hid my insecurities behind performance because I never felt good enough. Let me explain: I walked around with a secret and painful reminder in my heart. I honestly believed that if people knew about the abuse and rejection I experienced, they would run away like my Mommy and Daddy.

I rarely stood up for myself, and I was shy most of the time. I was bullied, talked about, and taken advantage of because I didn't have the courage to say: "No, you will not mistreat me." Why would I speak up? I allowed myself to be a doormat since I was four, and I watched my grandmother do the same thing for years. My personality and demeanor is just like the woman who raised me. People can sense my sweet, caring, and overly compensating spirit from a mile away. Most of the men I have dated admired me because of my "submissive and quiet" spirit. Children learn to imitate what they see.

I watched my grandmother raise myself and my siblings along with her great grandchildren. I watched her give her all to a church that took advantage of her kindness. She never said no even if it cost her in the end. Yes, it cost her. She dealt with disrespect and disobedience from rebellious children and grand-children. Despite how people treated her, I never witnessed my grandmother lash out or turn into a monster. She kept her cool and loved people anyway.

However, I wonder if she ever hurt or grew tired. Her love towards people reminded me of water coming from a fountain; it just didn't stop. I wonder if she cried at night when we would wake up and her car would be gone. I wonder if she cried when my brother continued to take her car and dabble in the streets. I won-der if she cried when I would kick and scream and tell her mean things when I didn't get my way. She never really spoke up, and when she did speak, she spoke with grace. Ironically, although she had the most beautiful soul I have ever witnessed, I knew she hurt. Her lack of sharing her "voice" transferred over to me.

The main motivation behind being a "yes" girl or rarely saying no comes from a detrimental belief: "If I say no, they will reject or dislike me. My deepest fear is to be rejected or disliked so to avoid experiencing those emotions and reactions from others, I will comply even when I don't want to." The Lord sees it as being a slave to man and fearing people above Him. It will keep you en-snared, always trying to make others happy when there is safety in the Lord (Proverbs 29:25). My desire to please cost me more than I imagined.

My low-self worth and self-hatred led me to trying mari-juana and having sex at 14. Although my sexual life was short lived, and I have been celibate for 13 years. I have compromised in other ways. My first mutual sexual encounter was with a man who was 7 years older than me. I wasn't head over heels or even attracted to him. Everybody was having sex, and he happened to show me some attention like the men from my childhood. I literally remember what I was thinking the night I lost my virginity: "This is probably the only man that will ever want me. He's wasting his time anyway. Nobody else wants me." Do you hear this worthlessness? Do you hear the heart of a young woman who does not see her beauty and value? I hated looking in the mirror because it reminded me that I was a reject. I felt so rejected by my parents that I internalized being an abomination to the outside world.

At 13 and 14, my sister and I sat down with my grandmother and she shared some exciting news with us!! After 9 years of being in New Orleans, we were headed back to New York to live with my mother. We were so excited; however, my grandmother gave us a warning: "It will not be what you think it's going to be." I never knew my mother was on drugs or that I was born a "crack baby" until we made it to New York in 2001. We moved to New York in the summer of 2001.

Shortly after we got there, my mother began using drugs again. My mother would use her food stamp money to buy drugs, steal the money our grandmother would send to us, and have other addicts in and out of the house. My mother eventually became physically abusive, and we had to be taken away from her. One day, my mother became so angry that she dragged me, pulled my hair out, kicked and punched me. I didn't have the courage to hit my own mother, so I took the beating. I remember being deeply hurt and confused by her actions. I didn't understand how a mother could verbally and physically hurt her children.

After the incident, I called my dad to pick me up. I remember it so clearly because once I got into my father's car, he looked at me and jokingly stated, "My poor baby." He made a mockery of my tears and showed no compassion for my hurt. I immediately stopped crying and accepted a false belief that day, "Crying is a weakness." Even as a newly 30 year old woman, crying in front of others is extremely hard for me. Every time the tears fall, I wonder if my vulnerability will be seen as a weakness.

I was 14 and my sister was 15 when we lived with my dad. It is utterly mind-boggling and amazing how the power of a dad can crush or elevate the minds of his children. It is a clear picture of the power of our Heavenly father. His love, grace, and goodness can elevate and crush us at the same time. However, his crushing and discipline produces character, hope, godliness, and perseverance. My father's presence and authority was strong in our home. He was the leader, and we were called to submit to his authority. We cooked, cleaned, and washed clothes. He taught us how to serve and comply to the wishes of a man.

Looking back on that experience, my father created a sense of reverence, fear, and awe in me for the male species. I don't have a hard time respecting and serving a man because it was ingrained in me to do so. However, my father also left painful writings on the wall of my heart that took me a while to overcome. One day he told me these painful words, "You will never be anything. You will be just like your mother." I don't recall why he said those to me. I don't remember being disobedient, yet those words stung. It hurt so bad and all I could do was cry. I didn't want to be on drugs and neglect my children. I can't imagine abandoning and abusing my children. I wanted more out of life, and my own father didn't see that. Stupid and broad were my nicknames. My father was an angry man, and my sister and I experienced his anger on a regular basis. As a result, I was insecure, gullible, and fell prey to the lies and whims of young boys and men. I just wanted somebody to love and accept me as a teenage girl, so I felt refuge in good friends, writing, reading, and poetry.

In high school, I was apart of the geek squad! My best friend was a light-skinned, curvy, skinny, and down-to earth Puerto-Rican beauty named MB. There were also three other girls I hung out with. MB and I were tight, and we loved the idea of being loved! We talked about love and boys all of the time, and we had a personal journal we would pass around between classes. We shared our frustrations, pain, and boredom with school. However, we found safety in writing down our feelings and listening to poetry.

It was a way of escape, and it felt exhilarating! Our journal entries sounded like diaries, and a way to hide our own miseries. In our journal entries, we shared our struggles with boys. It's crazy to read and hear how desperate I was for attention, and how naive I was to ill-intentioned young men. However, even at 30, there are some traits of that naivety still with me. My first journal entry was about a boy named D. He was a 16 year old Crip from Brooklyn. He was fine as wine with hazel brown eyes and a gorgeous smile! When I saw him, I couldn't stop staring. We connected instantly, and I visited Brooklyn frequently. My weakness even to this day is a good-looking man, and D. was a good-looking young brother with pretty eyes, a gorgeous face, and a beautiful smile. I was so glad that something that fine swung my way. I was hooked from the first interaction which led to phone conversations, hanging out, and eventually sex.

Right after we had sex, the phone conversations stopped and the avoidance began. I knew I played the fool. Moreover, he had a secret that he kept from me. He had chlamydia and gonorrhea. When I used the bathroom one day and I was hurting continually, I grew concerned. I went to the doctor and found out I had contracted a sexually transmitted disease. I was shocked because I believed D. when he said he was clean and didn't have anything. This painful experience led me to writing to my best friend MB whom I trusted and loved so deeply. I was longing to see D. after our sexual encounter, so I shared it with her:

I don't know why, but I just wanna see him again. I'm still not calling him until he calls me. I don't know why, but I just can't let it go personally. I think that he's doing it on purpose. He probably thinks he's too good for me. Well, if he calls me, which I highly doubt, I'll say, "Am I your girlfriend and are you my boyfriend?" If he says yes, then it will go on from there. If he says no then that's it. I doubt if he says no, but if he does, what can I do about it. Those eyes, damn those lips (mmm....). I want him so badly, but I know deep down inside I can't. He got me SPEECHLESS!

I was a lost Queen desperate for a young King to love me

who didn't know what love was. Puppy love, butterflies in your stomach kind of "love." We had no solid foundation, and were in heat kind of "love." Needless to say, my older sister Nikki talked to D., and his words were, "She knew what she was getting herself into." He didn't care. I was a hit on the hit list, and praise the Lord I didn't end up pregnant or with an incurable disease. Even during those times of hopelessness, lust, and confusion, God still protected me. MB and I wrote a lot in that journal because we trusted one another. We needed an outlet as we made sense of the crazy world around us. We eventually started going to Barnes and Nobles to read books in the aisles. Next, it was the Nuyorican Cafe in Manhattan and other poetry slams. We loved writing because it gave us a voice and helped us to make sense of everything around us.

During that time, we listened to conscious artists like Immortal Technique and Dead Prez. We gawked over amazing poets and artists who spoke their mind. I found a safe haven, and I used it to share my story with a Foster Care magazine called *Represent*. This magazine showed me that a creative young girl from the Bronx is indeed a writer, and her story and fight to live gives her purpose! After working with that magazine company, I knew I wanted to be a writer. I wrote poetry, dramas, and plays years later, but it started in high school when my mind was open to the world of reading and writing.

I had three dedicated teachers in high school that I remember vividly. One of the teachers names, I can't recall, but he was a white man who so happened to be my P.E. coach. He was always kind, and I remember him telling me that he wanted to see me do well and make it. His words were passionate, genuine, and strong! I will never forget those words because I knew it came from a sincere place. Real recognizes real. In other words, real people recognize genuine spirits, and his spirit resonated with me that day. My P.E. coach wanted me to soar, and I appreciated his passion. One thing about inner-city kids, our senses are very keen to bullcrap and sincere people. We can sniff out the real from the fake in a few seconds. We have to learn to be on the alert. We are forced to become skilled at navigating through the sticky and often hostile forest of the hood. My next two favorite teachers were Mr. Lawson and Ms. Williams. They were African American teachers who were passionate about Economics and African American History. They were excited to see us come into the classroom, and we were treated with so much respect and dignity as students. Mr. Lawson kept in touch with my sister and I outside of school, and he even took us to eat one afternoon. These two teachers became a safe place for my sister and I, and as grown women, we remember their love and investment.

Looking back over my life and childhood, I always felt an inner ache and belief that life had more to offer. It's funny how as an unbeliever I still had God's hand of protection on my life even as His enemy. Every situation and step was ordered and directed by the Lord. I knew I was different, but little did I know, the God of the universe was preparing me for a right relationship with Him. Your past is a gift and a blessing which ultimately points you to a God who will never leave you alone if you belong to Him.

INSECURITY

"You will never be enough" is a phrase I have told myself more times than I should have. There were a few moments in middle school and high school that revealed a sad reality: I was willing to do anything for love even if it cost me my dignity. I went to middle school in New Orleans, and I tried my best to stay out of trouble. I was in middle school in the early 2000's, and New Orleans was known for its crime and constant murders. I vividly remember receiving the news that one of my elementary school teachers was murdered. I was in complete shock! I couldn't comprehend how another human being can so heartlessly take another person's life.

In middle school, I wanted to be accepted and seen as beautiful. I wore makeup to enhance "my beauty"; however, I wished I wasn't overweight and more boys liked me. It's funny how African Americans promote and reinforce colorism in their own communities. New Orleans was known for favoring and uplifting light-skinned women while the brown and dark-skinned women took a back seat. I heard "Say Red!" more times than I wanted to hear. It proved to me that light skin women were more valued and seen as prettier even when some dark skinned girls looked better.

I was definitely "thick" for my age as an eleven year old in middle school. It was clear that I didn't miss a meal, and the food in New Orleans kept my taste buds churning. My mom visit here and there and eventually she stayed for sometime. In the time she would visit and when she did live with us for an extended period of time, I don't recall being called beautiful. She loved to mention how slim and attractive my sister was, and it made me dislike myself even more. I remember writing in my journal, " My mother doesn't love me because I am fat and ugly." I was determined to get the weight off in order to win her over and get the attention of young boys and men.

I starved myself literally. I barely ate, and I ran up and down the stairs in my home constantly. I remember one of our neighbors who happened to be a boy told me, "Quani, you would have dudes all over you if you lost some weight." His comment added fuel to the fire, and in one summer, I went from a size fourteen to a size four. My grandmother didn't know I was starving myself until one morning as I headed to school. I walked unto the bus to pay my fare, and as soon as I put the money in the machine, everything went black. I passed out on the bus, and my grandmother was called immediately. She took me to Shoney's Restaurant and encouraged me to eat. I needed that moment of understanding, and right after that, I became healthier and more stable. I began to eat more; however, I was still skinny because of the drastic weight loss. I dropped 10 dress sizes, so it took me a while to get that weight back.

During my middle school years, I was bullied and I also bullied a little girl. I was afraid of the popular girls, and I didn't stand up for myself the way I should have. I learned not to speak as a young girl and it showed up during my elementary, middle school, and high school years. Things began to shift after my sister and I moved out of my Dad's house when my little brother and sister moved to New York. Let me back track. After my mother beat me, my sister and I went to school the next day. My sister told our science teacher what my mother did to me, and we were escorted out of class. We were taken down to the office, and we had to tell the authorities everything that happened. We were then taken to the hospital where I took pictures, and we met our social worker Ms. B. She was a beautiful white lady who had the sweetest spirit in the world. Nikki and I were now apart of the foster care system due to the physical abuse of our mother. We moved in with my father, next my uncle, and two other homes after that. We were "foster kids"; however, the social workers we met along the way were absolutely amazing! It was in a foster care agency called "C.V." that I found hope and a voice.

This agency was geared toward encouraging, uplifting, and pushing youth in foster care to be and do their best. I was exposed to the world outside of "my hood" because of the activities set before me. (1) I received counseling, (2) met other teenagers in the same predicament, (3) experienced committed adults who loved me beyond my situation, (4) and applied to college and was awarded several scholarships. In my journey as a ward of the state, I met two of the most beautiful souls one could ever meet: Ms. B. and Ms. Perez. Ms. B was a wise older woman who saw beyond the surface of her clients. She definitely had the gift of healing in her veins because she pulled out things in people that they didn't even realize were there. She loved my sister and me so well. She invited us into her family, and we became more than clients. We were encouraged and inspired to use our story as a healing tool. Ms. B helped us to see that pain doesn't define you, but it tells a story of great triumph and intense victory. It doesn't make you who you are; it only sets you on a path to be the woman you were destined to be. She loved us beyond our story and pain, and my heart, mind, and soul will forever be grateful to have crossed paths with such an amazing woman. I pray that one day I get to share in the healing of others. She allowed us to meet her children, and she even invited us to speak at an event. Her footprint in our lives aided us to be victorious despite the obstacles around us. Recently, I wrote on her Facebook wall:

Chaquana: Hey Ms. B.! I am writing a book, and I am currently a teacher! I just wanted to say thank you for everything you've done for us over the years! We love you!!

Ms. B: Chaquana Muhammad Townsend, this message touches me deeply. I have loved you and your sister since the first time that I saw you. Your strength, resilience, passion, and loyalty to each other and family was amazing to me. I am beyond proud of both of you for breaking cycles and choosing to heal. I love you...

Even at 30 years old, Ms. B's words still bring healing to me. I am writing this book because I am choosing to heal. I am choosing to expose and uncover the pain in order to see the light. Shame no longer has a hold on you when you share what the enemy may use to quiet you. Shame can no longer whisper lies in your ear when you surrender to the Lord and say, "I will no longer allow the past to define me!" Shame has to flee when you tell yourself, "God works everything for the good of those who love him and who are called according to His purpose (Romans 8:28). Shame has to flee! Thank you, Ms. B., for showing me that healing is a choice. I choose to heal today and until the day I see the Lord.

Ms. Perez showed me what patience, care, and acceptance look like. I honestly believe that when God makes people in his image, he creates them to reflect his personhood. Ms. Perez was one of the most compassionate souls I've ever met. She was kind, understanding, and genuinely concerned about the well-being of others. Anytime you were around her, you felt valued and important. She loved my sister and me with open arms and no judgement. I remember being welcomed into her home and treated to dinner. I remember being close to a mental breakdown at 21, and she was there with me. I remember her going with me to the hospital and loving me through it. She congratulated me on my accomplishments, and she always believed in me which encouraged me to believe in myself.

Let's go back to my mental breakdown at 21. I had just graduated from Tuskegee University with honors, and I had a flashback that took me back to a scary place. Looking back on the event, I realize trauma will cause you to behave and act in ways that are detrimental for your well-being for the sake of survival. I was fresh out of college and headed to grad school. I was struggling with doing an internship with an inner-city ministry again or staying in New York.

Nonetheless, my mother invited her "guy friend" over to

my sister's house for the evening. When they walked in, I had a blanket over me because I was half dressed. I turned to look at her friend, and my legs started to shake and I became increasingly nervous. I got up with the blanket wrapped around me and walked into my sister's room. My entire body was shaking at this point, and I remember being molested at 4 or 5 all over again. My mother's friend had the hands of the young man who touched me the first time. His body structure reminded me of that same young man, and I was afraid. I called my mother into the room and asked her to have him leave because I didn't know what was happening to me. She became furious and eventually they both left. My body was still in shock, so I called two close friends to help me work through what was happening. That's when my healing journey actually began; it was the summer of 2010 when I realized I needed serious counseling because I had never dealt with the trauma of my past.

Ms. B became involved, and I was taken to a hospital to get evaluated. After the hospital visit, the nightmares increased and I ended up contacting a friend who was a social worker. The nightmares kept me from sleeping, and I was tempted to self-harm to rid myself of the pain. I was encouraged to contact a sexual abuse hotline to speak with someone to help me work through the inner turmoil. I also visited a friend who helped me in processing my internal and oftentimes debilitating and shameful pain. The facing of the pain began when I was 21, but its effects has had tremendous effects on my view of God and men. Throughout the course of my life, I have seen victories, defeats, and lessons that have shaped me into a resilient but scarred woman.

Nonetheless, God is intentional! He used my breakdown to show me the **need** for healing. I was angry, hurt, and trying to connect with a God that I didn't fully trust. He wanted to heal my broken and wounded heart, but I had to face the pain first. Contrary to popular belief, putting scriptures on top of your pain without honestly giving it to God is not true healing. Face it, give it to God, and then allow him to heal you. It takes a lot of courage to hand up your innermost thoughts and feelings to someone you are afraid will not still love you after the truth is exposed. However, our God can be trusted and He provides healing when we believe in His promises. I am reminded of the woman who was bleeding for twelve years. She went to many different doctors and had spent all she had, but she knew and believed that her healing would come from the ultimate healer. Lord, help us to trust you in the same way.

Mark 5:27-29: When she heard about Jesus, she came up behind him in the crowd and touched his cloak, because she thought, "If I just touch his clothes, I will be healed." Immediately her bleeding stopped and she felt in her body that she was freed from her suffering.

CHRIST INTERVENES

As a freshman at Tuskegee University, I was insecure, longing for acceptance, and eager to find peace and fulfillment. Sex was never my go to or struggle. Even though I wasn't a virgin, I knew I didn't want to give my body away to be used or taken for granted any longer. I was tired of giving sex in hopes of being loved. I slept with four guys from age 14 to 16, and I did not enjoy sex because I was emotionally disengaged. I wanted to be cared for outside of the physical realm, and unfortunately, I never received that. How could I expect something from young men who didn't know who they were?

One of my main reasons for not engaging in sex was ironic yet wise: I was afraid to go to hell because of my sin. Where did I get that notion? One of my friends in high school invited me to church consistently. I accepted her offer because I was longing for some type of hope and fulfillment. One day, her pastor said these horrific words that scared the living daylights out of me: "If you keep having sex and living for yourself, you will go to hell!" I made a vow that day, at 16 years old in Brooklyn, NY, to remain abstinent until I was married! Fourteen years later at 30, I remained abstinent with a few close calls and mistakes along the way.

I met Jesus at the end of my freshman year at 18 years olds. Before then, the Lord began working on me while I was in high school. Number one, a preacher scared me into fearing hell. Number two, I told my African American Studies teacher that I was going to find a good church home when I went to Tuskegee. That was all of Jesus speaking through me because my heart was so far from the Lord. I was smart, but I was living for myself. However, there was an emptiness that I couldn't shake. I was filled with self-hatred and shame due to my own sin and the sin of others. Shame filled my bones due to the sexual and emotional abuse, and I was longing to experience real, genuine, faithful, and enduring love. The Lord knew why he brought me all the way to Tuskegee University from New York City, and as I look back on it, it brings me great joy!

My transformation and conversion to Christ started at Adams Hall when the Lord blessed me to meet two of the most amazing God-fearing young women I've ever met: K. and A. Williams. They were my RA's also known as resident assistants. They loved the mess out of Jesus! They were unashamed prayer warriors and lovers of the word of God. They held a bible study in the dorm that I came to hear and there. They also held prayer sometimes throughout the week. These girls love for God intrigued me and pushed me to ask questions about who God was. I was also introduced to C. O. Ministries. This ministry held bible studies on campus and offered a summer project for students to grow closer to Jesus.

I went to church with A. Williams, attended Bible study and

prayer, and I even prayed to receive Christ, but I knew my heart was changed. I was searching and longing for a transformation, but it wouldn't happen until the end of my freshman year. C. O. had a summer project coming up. It was at the end of the school year in 2007. My plan was to go to summer school and learn about Jesus on my own. Nevertheless, there was a tug on my heart to get to know Jesus at the summer project. The summer project was geared specifically towards helping college students grow in their walk with the Lord, and my soul craved that. The love I didn't receive from my parents and the young men I gave my body to was the love I so desperately wanted! Little did I know that I would receive ten times more than what I could ever think or imagine.

I called Ms. B. to ask for her opinion. She was a woman I deeply loved and respected, and she knew me well. These were my words to her: "Ms. B., I can learn about God on my own. I want to graduate early, so I think I should go to summer school." Her words were strong and spoke volumes to my soul as a freshman in college: "Quani, I know you are smart and you can graduate early, but if you hate yourself and you're miserable, your education won't mean anything." Those words stung, but I knew what she was actually saying: "Go to the summer project, so you can be introduced to Jesus." That was one of the best decisions I've ever made in my life. I decided to go and the first couple of days I heard the Gospel so loud and clear! I was separated from God because of my sin, and the only way that I could be brought back to him was through His son Jesus Christ. I knew my sin separated me from a holy and righteous God, and I wanted so badly to know the God who did that for me. Another thing that sold me on walking with Jesus was the love and joy I saw in His children. A. Williams and K.

had love and joy unspeakable! The Christians that were apart of C. O. had joy that I knew nothing of. They loved God and one another like it was natural. I saw the light of the world inside of those brothers and sisters, and I told myself internally: "Whatever they have, I want it!" I wanted a reason to live because my former life sucked because it was a life lived for myself.

The project started on May 30, 2007, and I became a believer on June 2, 2007, in Piedmont Park in Atlanta. The project was held at Emory University in Atlanta, and we shared rooms with participants and leaders. I so happened to have built a relationship with a young woman by the name of K. Snead. Prior to the project, I went on a retreat, and I asked her several questions about the Lord. I was so hungry to understand the word and who Jesus was that I asked K. several questions. Several months after that, we were on the same project together and I trusted her leadership. On June 2, 2007, we had "Evangelism Training" which took place on a Saturday. I knew I wasn't a Christian because I know myself, and when God does something in your heart, you will know it. The night before I heard the Gospel again and even went to my room and asked Jesus to come into my heart, but my heart was the same. As the leader spoke about sharing "your faith" with others, I knew he wasn't talking to me. I was uneasy as he spoke, and I contemplated how I would tell K. Snead I wasn't a Christian. So as an unbeliever, I started praying: "Lord, please don't let me go with Kwajera. Lord, please don't let me go with Kwajera." I knew she was going to ask me questions I didn't have the answer to. I was determined to tell her that I wasn't a Christian, but I wanted to walk with Jesus because I understood the Gospel.

God is so strategic because right after I prayed that prayer, a sweet brother announced, "Quani, you are going with K. Snead!" I was disappointed and relieved at the same time. I was going to tell her the truth as we drove to Piedmont Park in Atlanta. I remember the conversation like it happened a few seconds ago. Before I get into my transformation story, I want to say this: "Jesus has been the sweetest thing I have ever known literally." When I contemplated cutting, suicide, and walking away from Him over the years, He was faithful. I have literally seen Him pull me out of depression, suicidal thoughts, and decisions that could have altered the course of my life. This love story is real! The realest love I have ever known, and I will shout it to the mountain tops: "I have found a real love! A love that is with you no matter what the cost!" My soul has found my truest love: Jesus Christ.

As K. Snead and I headed to the park, I spilled the beans: "I am not a Christian, but I understand the Gospel. I understand that Jesus died on the cross for my sins, and the only way I can get to the Father is through Him. I want to be a Christian." K. Snead stated, "We can pray now or we can pray later." I wanted to pray right then and there. In that moment, I asked God to forgive me for my sins. I asked him to change me and help me to walk with him. I remember both of us crying, and I vividly remember feeling a weight being lifted from my shoulders. It was like Jesus took the weight of the world off of my shoulders, and I had joy and peace that only He could give. I was genuinely happy for the first time in my life, and I was beyond excited to tell the world.

I was discipled that summer, and I learned how to spend quality time with Jesus. I learned to write out prayers to Jesus, study His word, and share my testimony and faith. C. O. set the stage for me to be unashamed of the Gospel, and I was discipled by several women over the years. I went back to Tuskegee's campus on fire and ready to share my faith. I evangelized consistently, attended bible study, and fellowshipped with other believers. I led a bible study on campus and invested my time into advancing the kingdom of God. In the summer of 2009, I was asked to be a leader on the very same project I became saved on! I accepted the request; however, I heard of two other opportunities that involved ministering to inner-city youth. After praying, seeking counsel, and the summer project in Atlanta ultimately being cancelled, I spent my summer in Montgomery, Alabama, with an inner city ministry. Two years after I became a Christian, the Lord sent me back to the inner-city to minister to children who were just like me.

This inner city ministry taught me so many amazing things in the summer of 2009. One thing the Lord revealed to me that summer was my racist heart. I did not like Whites because of jealousy and inferiority. I believed they were better, and I was beneath them to the point that I deeply distrusted them. I had a Caucasian roommate that summer who desired to build a relationship with me, but my walls were up. My truth and core belief about was race dominated my thinking: "You are white, and I am black. You will never understand!" The dislike and inferiority I felt around Caucasians came from what I watched on television and experienced growing up in New York as a teen.

Due to the conditions of the inner-city, I saw brown and black as bad and white as good. The media didn't help my thinking at all. The black people on television were loud, ghetto, uneducated, poor, ratchet, and lazy, and the whites were well-spoken, educated, and of the elite class. I hated being black, and I hated the people who I believed caused me to feel this way. I was convicted of my sin to the point of confession, repentance, and living communion at the altar to be reconciled to my sister and the Lord. The Lord placed me with a white roommate that summer who I coveted because of her privilege in America. I did not treat her as a sister, and by the end of the summer, I had to come clean about my sin. It was hard, yet the Lord broke the shackles of my racism. I was able to be honest with her and cry before her. The Lord restored my view of myself and my Caucasian brothers and sisters that summer, and I am forever grateful.

I learned that I had a passion for teaching, dance, drama and poetry, and loving on children. I fell deeply in love with the Washington Park Community, and the people that reside there. [1][2]My role with this ministry was to invest deeply in the lives of young boys and girls who lived in the Washington Park Community. I was a liaison between this ministry and the public schools. I was over the elementary or lower school portion of the afterschool program. During the day, I visited schools to check on students, ate lunch, met teachers, and built solid relationships with school principals and personnel. I fell deeply in love with every parent, every student, every intern, and everything that had to do with serving this community! Some days were hard and there were times students were disrespectful and parent relationship weren't always the best. However, I was willing to give my all for the cause of the Gospel. Long days, sleepovers, one on ones, discipleship, and learning and growing closer to the Lord through the highs and lows made me excited to go to work everyday. Something happened to my spirit when I was around those children. There was joy unspeakable! The good days definitely outweighed the bad, and I knew I was on a mission and on assignment. I was making disciples, investing in the academic success of the students, and loving on their families as well.

I grew in several ways as I worked in this ministry. I learned to love hard, persevere, and forgive. One of the students I grew close to goes by the name of Rockstar JT. When I first met him, I hit it off with him! Then as the school year progressed, he grew less fond of me to say the least. Most of the middle and high school students didn't like my stern approach, so they bucked against my authority most of the time. He and his best friend happened to be the students who made my job much harder. I was mocked, disrespected, laughed at, talked about, and simply mistreated just for the fun of it. I still stood my ground, but it took a toll on me internally. As crazy as it sounds, I grew to dislike JT and his best friend to the point of hatred. There was unforgiveness in my heart, and the Lord convicted me of my sin when I was around the two of them. JT professed to be a believer, so I called him out on things that were contrary to the word of God. I was consistent; however, the Lord began to speak to me about my relationship with JT.

I heard God as clear as day! The Lord told me to love on him and his mother. The Lord also pushed me to ask for his forgiveness in how I treated him and love him like a little brother. It was hard! Here I was a grown woman called to love on a teenage boy who disrespected me for the fun of it. One afternoon, I walked up to JT and asked for his forgiveness for my actions and heart towards him and it felt like a block of ice melted between us. There was a deep love and connection for him and his mom that blossomed. I fell in love with that family, and that same love still exist today. Although we don't talk as much as we used to, there is no denying the genuineness of that relationship.

I worked with the inner-city ministry from 2009 until 2015. Not only did I learn to love and forgive, I learned that Jesus loves me more than I could ever know. Let me explain why this is so important: One day like many other days, I gave simple in-structions to the students in the gym. I told them not to do some-thing, and shortly after I gave that command, they did the very thing I told them not to do. I was appalled, angry, and pissed off to be frank! The Lord spoke to me so clearly in that situation that it resonated deeply in my spirit: I have to remind you of my truth all of the time because you forget just like children forget to listen to the rules. That truth stuck with me and speaks to me today.

I was taught about the faithfulness of God as I served his kingdom. This amazing ministry was created with Washington Park as its target community. It was created to love, serve, save, uplift, and restore what sin left broken. This program was a God sent to the so called "least of these" according to societal beliefs and norms, and God loves the mess of my hood!! Yes, I am a proud resident of the Westside, and I don't plan on leaving unless my future husband decides to relocate. Please keep me here Jesus!! I love that God pursues his people and those that people deem unlovable. He died for the unrighteous which we all are no matter what side of town we live on. I am forever grateful for my time there, and it will forever have a place in my heart.

However, around 2015, the Lord began to burden my heart for the school system. As I visited elementary and middle schools, I met amazing, dedicated, and passionate teachers in the public and private school arena. I met teachers who loved their children, knew their needs, and paired up with the afterschool programs to aid in a child's success. I particularly grew a burden for African American males due to the countless cases of police brutality, and the disheartening mistreatment of black men and boys in society. It literally broke my heart and brought me to a place of confession and repentance.

I too struggled with loving the black man after countless acts of abuse and betrayal. I too held bitterness in my heart, and the Lord softened it after the two horrific cases of Trayvon Martin and Michael Brown. I was completely devastated that jail time wasn't given to any of the men who killed these young men. It crushed me, and I was determined to deeply love and cherish the black man and boy. I knew I wanted to teach by the end of 2015 due to several confirmations. On more than one occasion, I was told, "You should be a teacher." "Have you ever considered teaching?" One of my brothers in the faith called me a teacher. I knew the Lord was speaking to me, so I applied to Auburn University to get a Master's in English Education, and by the grace of God, I got in!!

Graduate school at Auburn was absolutely amazing! I met some of the dopest teachers and dedicated students. Three years later, I am still looking to finish my degree after taking a break due to teaching. Nonetheless, I learned how to teach through novels, how to relate to students from different backgrounds, and how to effectively teach and encourage reading in and out of school. My learning at Auburn and my experiences with the inner-city ministry equipped me to take my first teaching job in August 2016 at one of my favorite places to teach: a public, middle school on the Westside.

Due to my constant and consistent visits to the school, I was able to get hired through relationship building. It is utterly amazing how God strategically sets things up and hears the prayers of His people. I remember specifically praying to teach to a class of all boys, and the Lord gave me exactly what I asked for. I wanted to teach at that school in particular because of the relationships and connections I had formed with some of the teachers. Little did I know, God was going to use it for my professional and personal growth and spiritual maturity.

SAME-SEX
ATTRACTION

I have a motto that I live by in any work environment: "Be the best, work the hardest, and be the most passionate worker on the job. Lastly, love others even if it cost you everything." In any professional job I've worked, I have been passionate, one of the best, and worked my butt off even when I wanted to quit. One thing I observed about my dad was his work ethic. He worked hard when he worked, and he rested well when it was time to rest. This motto keeps you progressing and moving along in your career field, but it can have reverse effects that can cause burnout. As a believer my motto should come with these extra words: "Whatever you do, work at it with all your heart, as working for the Lord, not for human masters (Colossians 3:23)."

The crazy thing about my personality is this: Around unbelievers may aim is to be a light and stand out like I am supposed to, and that is what I do. I don't work to show my unbelieving how hard of a worker I am. I work from a place of this is what God can do when you surrender your life to Him. There is still an aspect of fear, but it is a healthy fear because I know my boss needs Jesus. However, in Christian settings, I tend to do the opposite. I want to prove to my boss that I am worth the hire like I try to prove to the Lord I am worth loving. Neither my bosses nor the Lord want me to kill myself mentally and physically to prove my worth, but I feel the need to earn their approval.

With my first teaching job, and I can honestly say this in confidence: I taught with all of my heart! Many days were hard; I dealt with disrespect and saw things that were disheartening; however, it was a mission field for me. I taught 7th and 8th grade English Language Arts. I knew every student's name, and I knew many of my kid's stories. I got to know them, and they trusted me. Some days they tried to buck against my authority, but I spent many mornings and afternoons talking to students, stopping by homes, and calling parents and students just to connect with them outside of school hours.

I loved teaching English! We learned so much history about minority groups, read extremely interesting stories, and my students did an excellent job on presenting their book projects! They were extremely funny, and I spent a lot of time laughing in between teaching. As I taught them, I asked personal questions and checked on them as well. I got to know students outside of my classes because I genuinely loved the brilliance and beauty this school had to offer. I was introduced to more students through teaching dance and helping with the after school program. My pod or team members became my family! We laughed, joked, and came up with strategic ways to teach our students. We saw our scores grow due to hard work, accountability, and a sincere commitment to the students we taught. Our students felt safe with us, and even when the days were hard, I knew they would come back around and apologize for misbehavior or misconduct.

Let me be honest: I loved working with the girls, but there was something that caused me great joy working with African American boys. I had minor behavior problems, and I grew close to many students both girls and boys. Nonetheless, I made it my goal to treat those black boys like Kings literally. Why did I do that? They get enough hate, criticism, and judgement. I taught around you Kings who were in gangs, held guns, robbed people, and fought for respect. Nonetheless, I saw Jesus. I saw young men who were smart, creative, passionate, and fighting to make sense of the world around them. I taught through that lens. I saw young girls longing for acceptance and fighting to love who they were. I understood what they were up against because I lived through the same thing at their age.

I longed for acceptance and approval from my family and peers. I longed to have my voice matter, and I wasn't going to add to their distress. Now, don't get me wrong: There were days I was pissed off by the lack of respect and laziness, and they heard it from me! I was that teacher to love on you and call you out for your laziness. I did not believe they were incapable of learning; I believed they needed to be challenged and held to a high standard. I was a fresh new teacher, so I am sure I made mistakes; moreover, we had a great time in class. We read poetry, and they wrote poetry. My kids were amazed by the cases of police brutality and the books we read! They began to love reading because their teacher cared about what she taught. Some days were hard, but they were all worth it.

Every teacher has a few favorites, and every teacher has that one kid that melts your heart away. The funny thing is this particular kid wasn't my student, but I so happened to cover his teacher's classroom and we met. I was calling the roll, and I called a student's name that wasn't there. Pickett responded with information on the student, smiled at me, and said: "I heard you were the nice teacher." I was sold! We made a small connection that day, and I continued to build a relationship with him throughout the year.

Pickett is probably one of the strongest leaders I have seen at his age. He stood up for students who were being picked on or taken advantage of. If he did something, people followed, and he protected the ones he loved and considered loyal. I called him King not Pickett for a reason. I told him over and over again: "You are a dynamic leader. You care about people, and people love to follow you. Use your leadership in good ways." I asked him about his future goals, encouraged him to do well in school, and talked to him about the Lord. He was receptive and always checked on me during the day. He gave me so much hope. God can make beauty from hard situations. His life wasn't easy, but he continued to persevere. I called his home several times to check on him. I stopped by his house to meet his mom and form a connection. It was a privilege to know a young King who was flawed, but yet so loved by the Lord.

The Lord used Pickett to show me a valuable lesson: "When students know you love them, they will do anything to protect you." Pickett knew my love for him was genuine, so in return, he protected me from students. I know this sounds weird, so let me clear up any confusion. He would walk into my class randomly and say: "Are you good Ms. Townsend?"

"If anybody messes with you, just let me know." One day I was outside with students and walked up and said: "Ya'll better know be messing with my favorite teacher. You good Ms. Townsend?"

He always gave me hugs and made my day pleasant. The days I had to call him out on his mess wasn't easy, but he listened because he knew I loved him. Pickett showed me that the way a teacher treats a student can determine that student's actions and perceptions. He was excited to tell me about his gains in math, and he was sent to my room once because I was one of the teachers he trusted. There were several other students who confided in me and loved on me as a first year teacher at Southlawn, and it blessed my soul. One experience with a female student, caused me to see that I am no different from my students. The only difference is age, and the working power of the Holy Spirit.

One of my 8th graders was exposed on Facebook performing an indecent act. She didn't know she was being recorded, so when it was exposed, she tried to commit suicide. She was embarrassed because of the comments of her peers. One day she came into my room to talk to me about the situation. I was in my late 20's, and I had never done what she did, but I knew what embarrassment felt like. More than that, I knew what shame felt like. I knew what it felt like to feel nasty or dirty because of an act you participated in. She was a gorgeous girl who liked the attention of boys. Most girls and women want to be wanted and found attractive, so I understood where she was coming from. She explained to me what had happened, and my question to her was: "What made you say yes to him?" Her words hit me like a ton of bricks: "I wanted to please him."

At that moment, I could have rebuked her and told her she was crazy, but I didn't. I told her I get it. My words were simple: "Girl, I am no different from you. One of my greatest sins and struggles is people-pleasing. I am afraid to tell people no because I am afraid of being rejected." I told her that what she did wasn't the wisest, but this can be a lesson for future references. I was able to connect with my students because I got to know the other side of them, and I was okay with it. I taught the whole student, not just the "academic" side of them, and I was grateful for the opportunity. Overall, the school taught me to connect holistically, and I am forever grateful. When I visit there now, I still know students because of the relationships I formed while I was there. Some of my former students still reach out to me because the bond we formed was genuine. That type of teaching kept me going everyday. I can honestly say that the discomfort didn't come from the kids; it came from my own sin and that of another.

So here's the part of the story I am trembling to tell because it shows a deep failure in my life. The Lord humbled me while I was at this school very quickly, and it was one of the darkest and most painful seasons of my life. I had teacher joy for sure because children have a way of making the sunshine when it's dark all around you. That's not cliche at all. When things were hard at the inner-city ministry and in the classroom, kids had a way of helping me to remember why I was there in the first place. They can be the calm to the storm. As a single woman, I know

God has called me to work with youth. I literally go to bed thinking about my students/scholars. My heart beats for them because at the end of the day, God calls me to make disciples and to love selflessly even when I don't like them in the moment. Let's go back to the original story. I knew I was going into a dark place. Before I was hired at this public school, I talked to a former teacher who warned me of the darkness. He was a strong believer, and I trusted his judgment. I assumed that the craziness would come from the children, but it came from the adults.

As a young attractive teacher, I found MPS to be toxic and detrimental. Most men and women in their 20's, 30's, and 40's are looking to find love or a romantic connection. I had no clue that men and women preyed on new teachers. I had no idea that people slept with people they worked with. I was completely naive to that part of the working world. When I got to my first teaching job, I was asked out the first week of school. I along with another young teacher became targets. I had turned down both married and single men while there because I knew where that would end.

However, if I am honest, I was vulnerable for a couple of reasons: "I had recently broken up with someone who I can honestly say I loved." I cut it off for immaturity reasons, and it just wasn't the right season for us. I needed to grow and so did he. Ironically, we are really good friends now, but that's for a later time. I still had very strong feelings for him, and we communicated off and on, yet the Lord had work to do. I was angry, bitter, and completely done with men. He wasn't the only man I dated, but I was so tired of being disappointed in men. I struggled with same-sex attraction as a Christian woman internally, but no one ever tempted me until I met her.

I have met beautiful women, but this girl was gorgeous! The enemy knows your weaknesses for sure. Sadly, she was my type: She looked like a man, but she was drop dead gorgeous. I convinced myself that a woman wouldn't hurt me like all the other men from my present and past, so this was safer. What a lie! I never suspected anything until things started to happen. The one thing I can say about the Lord that reigns true: "He will warn you when something isn't right." We as Christians must listen to the sound of His voice and obey immediately.

When I got to school, I met some of my coworkers, and I went about my business. I was not looking for anyone or seeking anything out honestly. This particular coworker added me on Facebook, and my first initial thought came directly from the Holy Spirit: "She either likes you, or she is observing your life because she sees your light." I had never spoken to this woman or interacted with her, so I knew she was watching for a reason. Warning number one. Naively, I walked up to her and asked her about her teaching career. I just wanted to be friendly because she was my Facebook friend. That interaction was extremely awkward. She didn't look me in the eyes, and she seemed very nervous. It confused me, so I just assumed she was an awkward person.

The next thing happened: She posted a status on Facebook about church options, and I was so excited to invite her to my church! I had no idea I was being baited in. People, including me, commented on her status. I knew without the shadow of a doubt she would be at church on Sunday. On Sunday, when I looked up, she was there. Not only was she there but so was my ex. They both told me they knew each other, and I just thought it was a coincidence. I thought nothing of it. Little did I know that she had gone through my pictures on Facebook and inboxed my ex-boyfriend just to ask questions about my personality. I sat next to her in church, hugged her, and couldn't believe she came to church. I felt like a missionary at school. My coworker, who happened to be gay, wanted to give God a try.

I am reminded of the scripture in James (1:13-15): "When tempted, no one should say, "God is tempting me." For God cannot be tempted by evil, nor does he tempt anyone; but each person is tempted when they are dragged away by their own evil desire and enticed. Then, after desire has conceived, it gives birth to sin; and sin, when it is full-grown, gives birth to death." I sensed an attraction from her, but I didn't want to jump the gun. However, once she confessed to having an attraction to me, I told her thank you for telling me. Then, I talked to her about the love of Jesus. I thought and actually believed I was strong enough to never give into the temptation of same-sex attraction, but I was wrong. I was in a vulnerable spot. I was hurt by men and utterly disappointed with "waiting on a man" to get himself together. I was angry, bitter, and completely discouraged, and Satan came to sift me like wheat (Luke 22:31-32). I told her that I too struggled with same-sex attraction, but my desire was to please Jesus and not myself.

Over the course of that school year, after be warned of backing away from her, I became emotionally involved. Nothing physical or romantic happened. However, just being around each other constantly and trying to be friends through conversations and text messages caused our hearts and emotions to become intertwined. I contemplated crossing over to the "otherside" because I was tired of waiting and God didn't seem to hear me. I wanted "my ex" and every other man who hurt me to see what they missed out on. She quenched my longing for affirmation, love, and acceptance. I liked the attention, and in the end, it cost me. I was convicted of the turmoil in my heart, so I told her the truth: "Yes, I am attracted to you and have strong feelings for you, but I am a Christian woman and I have to follow Jesus." The school year became hard due to the avoidance and conflict we were having. Words were exchanged, and we had to live with the reality of unmet desires.

That school year was great with my children; although, I had some behavior issues. Nonetheless, my relationship with her was so tense that I longed for a way of escape. I cared deeply for her and would even call it "love," but the jealous love of a heavenly Father continued to reel me in with His love and conviction. During that time, I lived with my pastor who happens to be one of my favorite people in the world! This man watched me cry my eyes out as I struggled with my attraction. He came to the school to visit me on more than one occasion. He talked to the young lady to encourage her as an image bearer in Christ, and most importantly, he called me out in love. His rebuke was hard, but extremely loving at the same time. He encouraged me to repent and change my mind about this young lady. He told me I was wrong, and that I would hurt the Lord deeply and the body of Christ if I gave into my sin. I felt like I was hit in the gut; however, his words along with the conviction of the Holy Spirit helped me on my journey to change my mind.

This sin had me bogged down, depressed, and contemplating if I should walk away from the faith or not. I was trying to justify why same-sex attraction was okay, but I could not back my sin up with scripture. It was clear that it was wrong, and I had to trust the Lord with the pain of unmet desires and continual disappointments. God's word was clear, and his wrath is for the man or woman who chooses to go after their on evil desires: *The wrath of God is being revealed from heaven against all the godlessness and wickedness of people, who suppress the truth by their wickedness, since what may be known about God is plain to them* (Romans 1:18-19). My coworker along with myself knew the truth, yet we suppressed the truth because of our own wickedness. As a witness for Christ, I not only defamed His name, but I hurt someone in the process. I should have never become her friend knowing my own struggle and hers. My heart and actions flirted with the idea, but I knew I had to turn to Christ.

It's crazy how Satan works because I knew I was brought to that particular school to minister to and teach young minds; nevertheless, I became distracted and wounded in the process. I had to face the reality that I was hurt and harbored unforgiveness toward one man in particular, and I was deeply dissatisfied with being alone. I never lost my teacher joy, but I lost my spiritual joy. I fought to come to church, and I wanted to believe that there was glory on the other side of this.

The Lord used Psalm 23 to help me to see His amazing love and hand on my life even when I wanted to give up and throw in the towel. I had people praying for me, encouraging me, and reminding me of who God was. Unfortunately, I hurt some friends in the process due to my isolation and internal battle; nonetheless, God restored those relationships. Psalm 23 helped me to see that the Lord was indeed with me as I battled my flesh, and the demonic forces I faced day in and day out. There was hostility and conflict, yet the Lord brought peace and cordiality to the situation. Although things were uncomfortable until the very last day of school, I was glad the Lord provided a way of escape and was beginning to restore my hope and joy in Him.

Listen to the words of God's servant David: "The Lord is my shepherd; I lack nothing. He makes me lie down in green pastures, he leads me beside quiet waters, he refreshes my soul. He guides me along the right paths for his name's sake. Even though I walk through the darkest valley, I will fear no evil, for you are with me; your rod and your staff, they comfort me. You prepare a table before me in the presence of my enemies. You anoint my head with oil; my cup overflows. Surely your goodness and love will follow me all the days of my life, and I will dwell in the house of the LORD forever (Psalm 23, NIV).

The Lord refreshed my soul even when I didn't deserve it. He gave me the strength and guidance to walk away from sin. He comforted me the many nights I cried out to Him when the pain became unbearable. He gave me an opportunity to repent and change my mind one more time, and for that, I am forever grateful. I didn't see joy on the other side; I couldn't see peace waiting for me, but He is a Father of good gifts. Although Satan almost had me, God came and snatched me! I am reminded of what Jesus said to Peter in Luke: "Simon, Simon, Satan has asked to sift all of you as wheat. But I have prayed for you, Simon, that your faith may not fail. And when you have turned back, strengthen your brothers (Luke 22:31-32)." Jesus was praying for me at Southlawn, and he continues to pray for me today. I am forever grateful that nothing or no one can snatch us out of the Father's hand (Romans 8:35-39).

REJECTION/PEOPLE PLEASING

Rejection feels like someone took a knife and lunged it into your gut. It feels like death if you allow it to. The older I get and the more in tune I become with myself, I see how my actions are a reflection of my thinking. After I graduated from Tuskegee University, I decided to pursue a Master's in Christian Counseling. My goal behind this endeavor was to grow in my understanding of how people operate based on their inner/core beliefs. In other words, I wanted to be better equipped to minister to the parents and children living in the Washington Park community. I knew the Lord was calling me to work with inner-city youth; moreover, I wanted to get prepared for it.

One thing I am learning about Jesus is this: "Whenever he prepares you for an assignment or task, he often uses that time to work deeply on you." As I pursued my Master's in Christian Counseling, I discovered some hard truths about myself that bleed into the fabric of my being and affect the way I view myself and others. These viewpoints turn into actions that take a mental, physical, and spiritual toll on my body. One of my core beliefs is this: "Something is inherently wrong with me, so in order to avoid rejection and exposure, I must please others no matter what it cost me and outperform everyone around me." The thought of this statement makes my heart ache literally, but this is how I live my life. I fear man more than I fear God:

Fear of man will prove to be a snare, but whoever trusts in the Lord is kept safe (Proverbs 29:25).

This belief developed when I was a young girl. Due to my parents' absence and continual mistreatment, once our relationship came to be, I internalized their behavior as a judgement on me. I always asked myself as a young girl: "Why doesn't my mother love me?" I often wondered if my appearance affected her love for me. I created a negative self-view and felt worthless because of the trauma I experienced sexually, physically, and mentally. Imagine being a young girl in high school searching for value and identity. Imagine waking up everyday wondering if your life matters. Self-help books became my remedy and reading for hours in order to escape my mental condition. I was a hard worker and used education as my source of value and significance. It's amazing how God used my time in grad school as a time of deep healing and restoration before I began working in inner-city ministry full-time.

As a full-time graduate student, I acted as a counselor and I was counseled as well. Those two years were some of the darkest and painful years of my life. It was there that I learned to forgive. I was deeply bothered by vulnerability and weakness. I didn't trust others too deeply, yet I longed to belong. I wanted significance, but I ached deeply. I remember crying loudly when I accepted the reality that my innocence was taken away from me as a young girl. I felt out of control every time a man had his way with me. Every touch took my voice away. I didn't know how to say no. I didn't know how to say stop. I grew to believe that being attractive and wanted was your asset as a woman. Attractiveness meant attention even if it was bad. I watched my mother and sister get attention, but it cost them. It cost them their peace, dignity, and self-worth. I wasn't any different from them because I bought into the lie too. I wanted men yet hated them at the same time. It was strange: Celibacy came at an early age for me because I knew I was tired of allowing my body to be used; however, I craved genuine attention, love, and respect. I learned to build friendships with young men at the age of 21 as a result of going through that program. The Lord used a couple young Kings to show me that not every man wants your body. I released the unforgiveness I carried for men for years and developed a better appreciation for them. They could be my brother and homie, and I wasn't in danger if I allowed them to get close. After years of uncertainty, I began a journey of healthy male relationships; even though, I had a long way to go.

I also had to face my disappointment with my mother and father. The compassion I have for my parents now is only something the Lord can give. I acknowledged their sin towards me, yet I understood the condition of their eternity. Let me explain: When a person is not connected to Jesus, they live to please their sinful man. Their actions are a direct result of the "god" they serve. You will either serve your flesh or your spirit. Listen to God's word on the two different natures: *Those who live according to the flesh have their minds set on what the flesh desires; but those who live in accordance with the Spirit have their minds set on what the Spirit desires. The mind governed by the flesh is death, but the mind governed by the Spirit is life and peace. The mind governed by the flesh is hostile to God; it does not submit to God's law, nor can it do so* (Romans 8:5-7). I was able to forgive my parents because I knew they were not controlled by the spirit of God. Their actions and mistreatment were wrong, but they were doing only what their nature produced.

Nonetheless, I acknowledged and faced the hurt and let it go. Crying and pushing through the pain and knowing that God cares for me in the midst of it, freed me tremendously. I couldn't hold them to a standard that was nonexistent for them. I had to release the pain in order to walk more freely as a woman. The Lord gave me a genuine love and respect for my parents; although, I disagree with their actions at times. I love my mother and my father, and I am no longer living as a victim of their neglect. It took a while, but from 21 to 23, I truly travelled down the path of forgiveness through intense counseling and prayer.

DADDY VOID

At 30 years old, the relationships that I treasure deeply are the ones I have with my dad and my pastor and friend Alonzo Brown. Although my relationship with my dad was rocky at times, it had the greatest impact on me. I honestly believe that your relationship with your earthly father has a profound effect on your view of your heavenly father. God designed that relationship to be a glimpse of His love for us; however, more times than not, our relationships with our fathers cause extreme trauma and damage. I can literally remember the very first moment I experienced great elation at the thought of seeing my dad and receiving a gift from him. I was four or five, and my sister and I were in New York. We met up with our dad, and he gave us matching sunflower dresses! I was so happy that my daddy gave me a sunflower dress because the image never left my mind. I couldn't wait to wear the dress that my daddy gave me since it proved I was thought about and special to him. That very moment created a joy and happiness that I don't remember experiencing again until my relationship with my dad was repaired years later.

After that pivotal moment, I don't remember interacting with my dad again until I was a couple of years older. He called one evening when my sister and I migrated to New Orleans, and I don't remember much of the conversation. I do remember the feeling I felt during and after the phone call. I felt uncared for, disregarded, and unloved. I was disappointed in my father. I didn't understand why he didn't see the need to stay connected to his children. That phone call was of no benefit because it clearly illustrated my father's disconnect with his children. At the age of 14 and 15, my sister and I lived with my dad after we were taken away from my mom. It was interesting to say the least because I learned some realities about my dad that caused great confusion and insecurities. My dad believed that women were to be completely submissive to men through cooking, cleaning, and service. I actually understood where he was coming from. The bible does call children to obey their father and mother (Ephesians 6:1). So if our father told us to cook and clean, that's what we had to do. However, he constantly reduced the woman's existence and role to serving a man. I never heard him mention the woman having her own identity outside of a man.

My sister and I constantly heard derogatory terms used about black women, and I felt less valuable than a man. My daddy made it clear that he was the man in charge, and we had to accept his authority even if it was exercised harshly. Instructions were given swiftly and authoritatively, and I remember being talked down to and yelled at frequently. My father called me stupid so much that I had to fight to believe that I wasn't. I vividly remember having a fit when a high school associate jokingly called me stupid. I went off and so did he because his words reminded me of a father who didn't shepherd my heart gently. I longed for affection and care, so I looked to other things to fill that void.

His treatment left me scarred and deeply afraid of any man

who was harsh or extremely authoritative. Men who were not gentle in their interactions with me were deemed unsafe and intimidating. I disliked aggression in men because it reminded me of the lack of care and emotional disregard my father showed in his interactions with my sister and me. I didn't want to be controlled or loved because I didn't make a mistake. I wanted to be loved because I was yours and you were mine. I longed for a father who treated me with kindness and celebrated my femininity, so there was a daddy void that I longed for someone to fill.

When I became a believer, I unconsciously viewed God as an authoritative Lord who wanted to punish me for my wrongdoing. I feared the Lord like I feared my father. Be good so you can be loved, grace and full acceptance is a concept I am just learning to grasp even after 11 years of walking with Jesus. It amazes me how your upbringing and small moments of pleasure or sin shape your entire outlook on life. The Lord had to deprogram my fear of men over the course of several years, and his work is still being perfected in me. I can genuinely interact with men, and the interactions are less difficult. However, there are still ways in which I allow myself to hold back or shrink around men who are in authority or authoritative. Submission and honoring a man comes easy to me because I was taught to reverence a man due to his leadership position. Although I haven't been perfect, I have learned to deeply honor and respect the position the Lord has put a man in despite the faulty view of inferiority and superiority that was ingrained in me.

My view of the Lord has drastically grown over the years. God's faithfulness to me has truly rocked my world!! The love that runs deep in my soul for the Lord comes from watching Him love and pursue me despite my mess. I do not understand why He loves me. I don't understand why His forgiveness is mine! I know without a shadow of a doubt that I belong to Him because His love never fails or runs out. He is good to me when I am up, and he is good to me when I am down. I know what it feels like to be loved deeply and wholly because God keeps rescuing me when my foot slips. Oh what a faithful father I have! The Lord has used my pastor Zo and many other men to show his great love and care for me.

The first time I interacted with Zo was as a freshman on Tuskegee University's campus. He was the most genuine person I had ever met. He was extremely kind, and he genuinely wanted to build a friendship with me as a campus minister. I honestly didn't have any discomfort or reservations about him. His gentleness allowed me to let my guard down and enjoy being around both Christian men and women. I remember telling him that he was the father that I wish I had. He was like a big brother, and he still is. He checked on me, encouraged me, and stayed consistent while I was a student at Tuskegee University, and we are still connected to this day.

I met him as a 17 year old freshman and over the years, he and his wife have seen my ups, my downs, and my comebacks. I have lived with him, and I actually feel apart of the family. If the Lord does allow me to get married, I want him to be apart of the ceremony. His leadership, covering, and encouragement over the years has kept me encouraged and steadfast when my heart wanted to do otherwise. I am grateful for his life, and his leadership over the years.

PERFORMANCE JUNKIE/I TEACH

I know with all of my heart that God has called me to teach African American and minority boys and girls. There is a joy and excitement that children bring me that I cannot explain. Their smiles, innocence, curiosity, honesty, and sinful nature intrigues, excites, and compels me to love in ways that I never could imagine! They are definitely my cup of tea, and my joy on this side of heaven. However, as a third year teacher (one year in public, and a year in a half in private), I had to figure out along the way that obedience and walking in your purpose God's way brings more joy than anything else. Teaching cannot be about "performance" or the "approval of man," but it must be about God's kingdom and purpose for the minds you are educating. Teaching became joyless when I took my eyes off of Jesus and placed it on "performance." Let's start at the beginning.

I remember when the Lord started to put a burden on my heart to teach. It began in 2015. As a parent and school liaison between the Montgomery Public School and an inner-city ministry, I watched amazing, dedicated, and competent public school teachers teach young minds. I witnessed excellent classroom management, stern conversations, potent organizational skills, and a genuine heart to educate disadvantaged children. On the flipside, I have also witnessed honest frustration, discouragement, disrespect, and a lack of care and concern for the minds of our students/children. As I went into Southlawn Middle School, Bellingrath, Carver High School, T.S. Morris, E.D. Nixon, and Montgomery Christian School, I began to be burdened with how to play a significant role in the life of boys and girls for long periods of time. Although I worked with children in an after-school program, I wanted more access to them. With prayer and several confirmations, I left Common Ground to pursue a career in teaching.

Whenever the Lord gives me an assignment or a yes, he will give me clear affirmations through His spirit, a lack of peace until I move, the wisdom of others, and the opening and closing of doors. As I visited T.S. Morris in particular, I absolutely loved the drive and dedication of the teachers! I was amazed by their performance and desire to work with me. One day I was working with the librarian, and she asked me a question: "Have you ever considered teaching? You are great with children." I looked at her and said, "I have. I am actually considering going back to school to get a degree in education." I knew that was confirmation from the Lord that my desire to go back to school to teach wasn't a coincidence. The next confirmation I received came from Mr. Brock, the headmaster of VCA. He addressed me as a teacher. I chuckled inside because I knew the Lord was tugging on my heart to resign from my full-time job and pursue the field of education. I stepped out on faith and decided to apply to Auburn University's English Education program, and I was accepted shortly after. I knew the Lord was telling me to go because He opened the door for me to pursue my degree.

I knew the Lord was calling me to teach in the public school. I had completely fallen in love with one public school, literally. I loved the children and staff I came in contact with. Moreover, I watched two dynamic teachers master the classroom. I knew one of the teachers knew the Lord based on her interaction with the students. She was dynamic, and her students seem to feel safe with her. As I walked the halls and observed, I saw the bad but I also saw good. I begged God for a job at Southlawn and due to my constant communication and interaction with the school, the Lord surprised me one day.

I decided to move back to Montgomery and commute back and forth or possibly transfer to AUM. My living situation didn't workout in Auburn, so I asked my pastor to me stay with him. He and his wife allowed me to live with them, and I started job hunting as soon as I moved in. I applied to different schools in the city, and one day, I ran into the current principal of Southlawn Middle School. An employee introduced me, and I stated that I was finishing my degree and was interested in teaching at his school. He encouraged me to come to see him after I receive my degree. A day or two after our initial conversation, I received a phone call from him inviting me to interview for an English position at the school. I was hired instantly, and I walked into the classroom the same week. I prepared an introduction lesson, but I did not know what to expect the first day. Teaching was natural for me. I loved Southlawn instantly because I spoke their language.

Let me explain: I love African American culture! I love the

music, fashion, creativity, and realness my people possess. I was once a child growing up in the hood, and as an adult, I knew I would live in the inner-city no matter what career I chose. I know, understand, and believe in inner-city kids period! I do not believe the lie that they are not as smart as other races. I am an inner-city kid who excelled in school and received several awards and scholarships to attend college. I had adults who poured into and told me I was great, and I believed them!! I brought that same tenacity and belief with me into the classroom, and I had a blast with my students as a first year teacher.

I was given 7th and 8th grade English to conquer. On top of that, I was a dance coach because of my love for dance. I learned how to execute lesson plans, teach standards, and manage children. Southlawn was definitely challenging, and I had to learn how to navigate tough situations. I was cursed out, pushed, and disrespected on several occasions, but I still held my ground. I taught passionately, contacted parents, stopped by houses, and encouraged my children to love their heritage. We read books and stories, listened to poetry, and learned a lot of words and techniques in order to get better in reading. I learned along the way as a new teacher, but I had joy doing it! Some classes were more challenging than others, and I disliked some of the extra duties that were put on us as teachers.

Nonetheless, I fought to be the best teacher I could be. I was punctual and did everything I was told. Although I wasn't perfect, I knew I wanted to be an example to my coworkers and students. I was the Lord's ambassador, and I knew I had to represent Him. I was committed to treating my students as Kings and Queens made in God's image, so when I messed up, I knew I had to make improvements.

The hardest thing besides my situation with my coworker (same-sex attracted coworker) was the failing/low test scores which was a reflection of a lack of accountability within the school system, and the mentality of the children. Although I loved my babies, their environments and mindsets reflected a lack of parenting, an ignorance of how great they were, and a commitment to a culture that dehumanizes them. Most of my children didn't know Jesus, but they were some of the sweetest, funniest, brilliant children I knew. Some of my students were extremely bright while others struggled in reading. Nonetheless, they met my standard, and some progressed throughout the year.

I was taken aback by the homosexuality flooding the halls of Southlawn. Most of the girls were gay or bisexual and although I struggled with it myself, I knew it was a tact of the enemy to keep their eyes off of Jesus and on their desires. Sex and gangs were rampant throughout the school, so I made sure I prayed for my children and shared Jesus with them. I was unashamed of the Lord, so I had many conversations about Jesus because He was the only hope I could offer them.

One situation sticks out in my mind. The Lord used this situation to show me how I am no different from the children I teach. The only reason why I am not gay or sleeping around is because I know what I am worth, and I know the pain and consequences of sin. When I want to give in, I think about the pain, consequences, and disaster that awaits me on the other side. When I get caught up, the Lord constantly brings me back to my senses because He is committed to me. I will call her Queen. One of my smartest students didn't come to school one day, and a student asked me, "Ms. Townsend, did you hear about Queen?" I said, "No, what happened?" The student informed me that she was caught on Facebook giving oral sex to a young man. I also learned that she tried to hurt herself as a result of being exposed. My heart was broken.

When she finally returned to school, she came to me and asked, "Ms. Townsend, did you hear what happened?" I looked at her and said, "You can tell me." She told me that she was hanging out with a guy she knew, and he asked her to perform oral sex. She liked him, but she didn't want to do it. She gave in; however, she did not know she was being recorded. I listened quietly, and I asked, "What made you do it?" She stated, "I wanted to please him." When those words came out, I felt conviction and sadness all at the same time. I told Queen, "You know what's funny: my biggest struggle as a Christian is pleasing people. I say yes when I really want to say no. I please people even if it cost me in the end. I have to ask God to help me every single day." We talked some more, and I encouraged her. That moment was pivotal for me because it proved that the only difference between myself and my student was I knew Jesus and happened to be several years older. Even with Jesus, I could be in the same circumstance. I still saw beauty in the midst of extreme chaos.

I decided to leave Southlawn due to the coworker conflict, and the Lord was clear about where I was going next. Anthony Brock, the founder of Valiant Cross Academy, approached me on different occasions about teaching. We stayed in touch while I attended Auburn and taught at Southlawn. He was such a huge encouragement to me and still is to this very day. I knew I had to leave Southlawn for mental health reasons, so I began praying about what was next. One day, I prayed and asked God to make it clear if He wanted me at Valiant Cross Academy. I prayed for specifics. I prayed that Mr. Brock would inbox me and make it clear that he wanted me to work for him. Shortly after that, Mr. Brock inboxed me and made it clear that he wanted me to work for him. God has a sense of humor!! I went up to the school a few times, and I signed a contract for my second year of teaching. I was so excited!!

V.C.A. has truly taught me the power of excellence, classroom management, and drive. I would not be the teacher I am today without the help of the Brock Brothers. The passion, drive, commitment, and love these men have for education and African American and minority boys amazes me. I have truly found a family and home in Montgomery. The Lord began giving me a deep burden and heart for African American boys after the shooting deaths of Trayvon Martin and Michael Brown. My heart and actions were geared toward making every brown boy or man feel like a King in my presence. I was overjoyed to work with African American boys and prove to them and the world that excellence was easily within their reach.

The trainings, accountability, high standards, school visits, coaching, and evaluations pushed me to be the best teacher that I could be. I have literally seen scholars reading scores improve drastically through analyzing data, strategic teaching and planning, data driven instruction, consistent classroom management, and strong dedication. I received the best training from the best leaders, and I am forever thankful. I know what it looks to produce excellence and push scholars/students to meet your expectations. However, it came with a cost. One of my greatest sin struggles is working wholeheartedly as unto man. I am a man-pleaser, and I live for the approval of others. I want to be the best and get everything right the first time, so the concept of grace is hard for me to receive and accept. Perfectionism looks good on the outside, but it can leave you emotionally, physically, and mentally exhausted.

My first year at VCA was excellent! I taught with all my heart, mind, and strength, and the test scores made that evident. Nonetheless, I was working long hours that cost me a lot of sleep. Some nights I would get 3, 4, or 5 hours of sleep due to my desire to read, memorize, and master everything. If I got six hours of sleep, I was doing really good on that particular night. Don't get me wrong: I don't need much sleep to function, and I do believe there are times when you have to sacrifice sleep on behalf of others; however, my excellence was turning into workaholism which was causing great anxiety and a lack of joy.

I had to spend less time with friends and the body of Christ in order to meet the standards of excellence. I loved teaching 6th, 7th, and 8th grade, but it required a lot. I am not a "cutting corners" person, so whatever is asked of me is completed no matter what it costs me. I would be at the school after 8, 9, and sometimes 10 o'clock getting things done. I would also arrive extremely early in order to master my craft. Honestly, I did the same thing at Southlawn, but I didn't stay as late since the school day was shorter. When I had to attend counseling in order to make it through the school year, I knew my anxiety was high. One day, I had to pray myself out of a panic attack at the thought of not getting all of my work done.

The workload was often heavy as with any school. When teachers bear the spiritual and academic portion of a scholar's life, we often spend more time working than being with our own friends and families. Working with a minimal amount of personal time caused me to be frustrated, sad, short, and mentally exhausted. If I am honest, I made performance and looking good my idol and it cost me. I often led out of intimidation and a lack of grace because I wanted to produce perfection for my bosses, a good evaluation at the end of the year, and a great reputation with visitors. People come and marvel at the product, but they don't see the work that goes into it. I spent several hours in counseling due to a fear of failure, fighting extreme anxiety, and wondering if I should call teaching quits. Of course every school deals with defiant children, so carrying that pain was apart of the job too.

In my first and second year, I had to fight for joy every single day. There were days I didn't want to go to work because I was fighting to believe that I was good enough. I lived to make a "proficient" or "excellent" on my evaluations that it became about "looking good" and "performance." I taught out of fear of making a mistake, so there were times when I led out of a lack of

I felt pressure to perform, so I put that same pressure on my

though I had some really amazing days at VCA, I didn't

know how to be Chaquana Townsend. I was tense and just wanted to dot every I and cross every T. I was fighting depression and whether or not I should leave teaching the first semester of my second year. I had just gone through a traumatic dating experience, and the pressure of work became too much for me.

I started praying, fasting, and seeking counsel on whether or not I should continue at VCA. Moreover, I missed working with young girls and boys and using writing and dance as an outlet. Teaching started to feel too heavy, and I began to feel convicted about making disciples and really knowing my scholars/students. There were families and scholars that I was extremely close to, but there were some I wanted to get to know. When I was at Southlawn, I taught dance and two grades, yet I literally knew all of my students outside of the classroom. I built such a strong relationship with them that behavior issues dissipated. I was no longer happy at VCA, and I knew God was calling me to leave.

I wrestled with God in prayer because I didn't want to leave. I went back and forth and tossed and turned most nights. I asked myself, "Why?" over and over. I told myself I could push through it, and I told myself to leave. I knew I hit my breaking point when I cried my eyes out one night the last month of school. I was tired of performing; I was tired of living to look good for "the outside world"; I was tired of being fearful of making a mistake. I couldn't see Jesus anymore; my eyes were on "performance." I was holding onto my sanity through prayer, fasting, and counsel, and due to hard circumstances personally, I was suicidal. It was no longer healthy to stay in a "performance" state of mind. I needed grace, freedom, and wholeness, so I obeyed the voice of the Lord and decided to leave.

When I told the Brock Brothers, they were so supportive and encouraged me as their sister in the Lord. They understood my struggle and loved me until the end. I talk to Anthony Brock on a regular basis, and they have said on more than one occasion, "Let us know if you need anything." I made a commitment to stay connected, and they have kept the door open. Mentally, I was in a bad head space, and I know the Lord has to do some work on me. I am going back to Southlawn because I felt connected deeply to my students. I absolutely love working with inner-city youth. I connect well with brokenness because I know I can be a light. The same drive and passion I brought to VCA will be brought to South-lawn. I am a better teacher and more aware woman due to my time at Valiant Cross Academy, and my life will never be the same.

IDENTITY/GRACE

My struggles at V.C.A., Southlawn, and in life in general come from the lack of understanding grace and identity. If I understood the amount of love, commitment, and forgiveness God bestowed upon me, I wouldn't live to be accepted by man. It is utterly amazing to me the connection and love I have for inner-city children because I am one of them. I thrive at Southlawn because I understand what it looks like and feels like to be in the wild fighting to survive. I know what it feels like to want a solid love only to get lust and addiction under the guise of love. I understand what it looks like to be considered "the bottom" when your heart, personality, and who you are as a person is beauty at its core. I am a broken woman, completely in need of a heart transplant and healing in so many areas. I have gone left when God said go right. I have denied Christ with my thoughts and actions, yet for some reason, he puts up with me.

After several years of walking with the Lord, I see the importance of having a solid family background and parents who walk with Jesus. Even at 30, I have to fight the lie that I am not enough. I literally have to affirm myself through prayer and God's word every single day. If I am not allowing God's word to be my comfort, sadness and disappointment will overtake me. I wasn't affirmed by my parents until I was much older. I didn't have a man telling me I am enough in and of myself. I was constantly torn down and literally treated as if my existence was beneath a man. I was brought up to believe that my physical features were the most important thing about me. As much as I love my dad, he exercised his authority to keep us in line. He taught me to be obedient especially to the opposite sex even if it was uncomfortable. Grace and kindness came later on in my life, but the damage had been done.

The thought that God loves me unconditionally is a new concept to me. Every single time I hear about what Jesus did, it makes me tear up. His love is overwhelming, and the most beautiful thing I have ever experienced in my life. I am his daughter, friend, and bride. When I try to use other things to fill my sadness and depression, he reminds me that he is all I need. I am valuable because thousands of years ago, he chose me before the foundation to be holy and blameless in his eyesight. He chose me to have a calling, a purpose, and an identity. I am his, and he is mine. He walks with me when life is sweet, and he walks with me when life is overwhelming. He is there when I hate who I am because I am carrying shame for what was done to me and what I did. He allows me to mess up, and he convicts and encourages me to look to him. When I think of purpose, identity, and grace, my mind first goes to Genesis 1:26-27: "Then God said, "Let us make mankind in our image, in our likeness, so that they may rule over the fish in the sea and the birds in the sky, over the livestock and all the wild animals, and over all the creatures that move along the ground."

I was made to look like Jesus and rule. I was made to reflect ˈ can speak, create, think, and influence others because

I was created by a speaker, creator, thinker, and an influencer. I was made to be royalty; I was made to make beautiful things and be beautiful because God makes beauty. Another scripture that comes to mind is further down in Genesis 1: "God blessed them and said to them, "Be fruitful and increase in number; fill the earth and subdue it. Rule over the fish in the sea and the birds in the sky and over every living creature that moves on the ground." With this command, I am called to increase in number. I have a purpose as a Christian woman, and that purpose is to make disciples and reproduce young men and women that reflect Jesus. My life was made to show other people the beauty of God. I am his masterpiece created to do a specific task: "For we are God's handiwork, created in Christ Jesus to do good works, which God prepared in advance for us to do (Ephesians 2:10)." I was crafted by the maker with a purpose and for a purpose. I am only walking in his purpose for me. What an amazing God!

I was made by him and for him in order to show off his handiwork. My brother and sister, your light and life as a believer cannot be hidden: "You are the light of the world. A town built on a hill cannot be hidden. Neither do people light a lamp and put it under a bowl. Instead they put it on its stand, and it gives light to everyone in the house. In the same way, let your light shine before others, that they may see your good deeds and glorify your Father in heaven (Matthew 5:14-16). I wasn't made for myself or for the pleasures of this world; I was made to point God's creation right back to him. I am enough because God doesn't do half work. God looked upon his creation in Genesis, and he said it was good (Genesis 1:31). The thought that God looks upon me and smiles warr my heart ten times over. He loves me because it is who he is delights in his creation, and for that, my heart is glad. I've always wanted to be delighted in, and now, I am reassured that someone loves me for who I am. Grace frees me while fear traps me. Grace heals me while lies entangle me. I am free to be creative, outgoing, cheap, funny, and compassionate Chaquana because God made me that way. His grace says I don't have to work to be loved, forgiven, and accepted; I am already loved, forgiven, and accepted: "For it is by grace you have been saved, through faith--and this is not from yourselves, it is the gift of God--not by works, so that no one can boast (Ephesians 2:8-9)."

STRONG TOWER AT WASHINGTON PARK/ STEADY FIGHT

I am beyond blessed to be a part of the church I attended. Flatline Church at Chisolm is an extension of Strong Tower. I am deeply loved and in a way that I have never been loved by human beings. They are my family because to call my church my friends would be an insult and understatement. I have built solid relationships and friendships with strong believers who constantly and consistently push me towards the Lord. There is a sisterhood and brotherhood that extend beyond race, socioeconomic status, and marital status. We are connected and completely one as God's word indicates, " For even as the body is one and yet has many members, and all the members of the body, so also is Christ. For by one Spirit we were all baptized into one body, whether Jews or Greeks, whether slaves or free, and we were all made to drink of one Spirit" (1 Corinthians 12:12-13). I have been a member of Strong Tower at Washington Park since 2012, and I have had my extreme highs of walking with Jesus and extreme lows. It is at this church where I grew deeper in love with Jesus through the conviction of His word, His people, and through serving. My pastors in particular have stuck closer than a brother. My closest sisters have encouraged me when I was knocked down by the cares of life.

I can think back to 2015 when the Michael Brown verdict came out. I was living with my sister in Christ and best friend K. Hartzog.. The story of how we met is quite simple. We actually met in 2012, three years prior. She started coming to Strong Tower after I began going, and we introduced ourselves one Sunday morning. Somehow, through the grace of God, we hit it off and became friends. Eventually, after a year of living alone, she became my first roommate when I was ready to enjoy community and fellowship in my home. God knew what he was doing when she became my dear sister, friend, and roommate. Our personalities just clicked. We both loved Jesus like crazy. We both loved our church, and we loved serving and loving on others. She and I didn't make decisions apart from each other. We cooked for each other, and we served our neighbors well. We prayed for each other, encouraged each other, and cared for each other deeply. The closeness we shared was God-given, and I was so grateful for her friendship. We both felt strengthened and encouraged by the friendship because of our love for one another.

My favorite thing about living with her was her desire to love and serve others. She often cooked and served our neighbors selfishly. Her honesty with me was genuine and heartfelt. I knew the Lord used that time of living together to show me His kindness. We had countless talks when life was good and when life was hard. When we started dating and opening our home, I appreciated the accountability. Our pastor lived right next door, so nothing was hidden or kept away. We lived our lives out in the open, and I can honestly say that we enjoyed the fellowship of the saints and the community of Washington Park. When heartbreak and disappointment set in, we comforted one another and prayed that God would hear our cries for healing. One weekend in particular was hard for me. It was 2015, and I was working out at the downtown YMCA. I remember watching the uproar in Ferguson, Missouri, over the death of 18-year-old MIchael Brown. I saw burning buildings, people marching, and the pain and cries of a mother who had lost her son. I also saw Michael Brown's body lying in the street uncovered. I saw video footage of him taking a bag and shoving a store clerk as well.

As I watched this footage over and over, my heart became saddened and enraged. I kept asking myself these questions: "Why was he killed? Why didn't the officer just shot him in the legs? Did he have to die? Why is he being criminalized? Why are people so judgmental? Why did a mother have to lose her son?" I was so hurt and still healing from the Trayvon Martin verdict. I was crushed that the black man was so unloved, hated, and completely emasculated by society. Most importantly, I thought about his mother. I remember house sitting that weekend going into a new week, and I caught the footage of Michael Brown's mother, family, and friends waiting to see if officer Darren Wilson would be charged. When the verdict came out that he would be let go, the cries of this mother were heart-wrenching and deeply painful. She covered her face, and the roaring of disappointment escaped her beat up soul. I lost it! I wrapped myself in a cover and held on for dear life. My entire body ached, and I felt like I had lost a son or relative.

When I got to my home one day that week, I remember walking into the house and getting under the covers like once before. I just cried. I felt helpless. I didn't understand why an officer who knowingly killed a young man didn't get charged. K. Hartzog, who happened to be home, walked into my room with some water and just sat there with me. She didn't say any profound words or read the Bible to me. She was just with me, and the Lord used that to help me process my pain. Her friendship is something that I am grateful for and blessed to have. Now, I get to share in her matrimony and witness God's faithfulness to her. Through her highs and lows of dating, God blessed my friend with a life partner! Her love for God, His people, and her future husband convicts and encourages my soul. I praise God for my sister and friend.

I don't think there are words for how much my brothers and sisters in Christ have loved me through the good, the bad, and ugly times. If I could share a few stories, I can think of specific incidents where I was rescued, encouraged, and shielded by men who love me like I was their own. I will start with my pastor T. Jones and his wife. Number one, it has been an honor and privilege sitting under his leadership for the past 7 years. I have seen a remarkable picture of what it means to live for Christ and to make disciples of all nations. My pastor and his wife have sacrificed so much to shepherd the body of Christ, and I am forever thankful for their service and friendship. There is one area of my life that T. has shown up time and time again, and that is in my dating life. Not only that, he has encouraged me as a sister in the Lord to constantly fix my eyes on Jesus and not the things of this world. I can think back to when I first joined the church in 2012.

T. has always encouraged me to use my God-given gifts to glorify God. Anytime I wanted to serve in church by teaching dance or drama for the Christmas play or host a Mic Check night filled with rapping, dance, drama, and poetry, Terrence was always behind me 100%. He has also been very honest with me when my choices concerning the opposite sex lacked discernment and wisdom. In this area of my life, I have blindly believed the words of men and allowed my heart to go deeper than it should. T. has graciously rebuked me and sat down with men who desired a relationship with me, but their walks with God did not produce the necessary fruit. Recently, my pastor stepped in when a situation became out of my control and fear gripped me and the young women living with me. A guy whom I recently dated happened to be standing outside of my window one night after we had ended the relationship. I screamed and ran as fast as I could when I noticed him outside the window. My roommate called the police and my pastors were next on the list. T. picked up, and he came to my house as soon as he could. He drove around the house to see if he saw anything, but no one was there. Out of fear, my roommates and I spent the night at his house.

I was embarrassed, hurt, and heartbroken all over again, and Terrence never condemned me. He lovingly told me the truth and encouraged me when I wept over the disappointment and sin. Everytime I dated a man, he knew it wouldn't work out, so he graciously gave me his words of wisdom and loved me when what he had predicted came to be. Although I felt hopeless and beat up all over again, T. reminded me of God's grace to me and his commitment to love me as a brother and pastor.

I can vividly remember two phone calls that consisted of heartbreak and a situation that sprung up out of nowhere. T was there and always helped me to see that it was God's way of showing me I needed to focus on Him and not on what I didn't have. For seven years, he has been committed to my spiritual growth through prayer, counseling, encouragement, and several meetings. When I struggled with my battle of same-sex attraction, he walked with me through that storm. I remember fighting internally with the desire to go to church because I contemplated loving Jesus or being gay. Terrence called me to make sure I was going and offered to pick me up. Throughout the years, through the good and bad, he never allowed me to slip through the cracks, and I am forever thankful!

There are so many couples and friends who have been there for me through the ups and downs of life that I am forever grateful for. I think of many other brothers and sisters in the faith that have prayed for me and encouraged me when life was difficult. Recently, I had a brother step into my life in ways that literally helped me through one of the most difficult times in my life. K. Adams and his wife, Mrs. Adams, walked me through my last semester at my old school.

K. Adams and I became extremely close through talks, encouragement, phone calls, text messages, and home visits. This brother encouraged me when I was struggling with leaving my job due to my struggle with performance and the grace of God. He gave me insight on relationships when I had to make a choice to walk away from someone who was unfaithful. When I was struggling with extreme anxiety to the point of walking away from the Lord and suicidal thoughts, K. Adams consistently called, texted, prayed for me, and even fasted on my behalf. Out of nowhere, a meeting was held with my counselor, pastor, and Keelan concerning my suicidal thoughts and what I knew God was telling me to do. God was telling me to move on from my job and pursue Him wholeheartedly with my life. I signed a paper for accountability purposes stating that I will not hurt myself and will commit to calling three people if I am struggling. I was completely blown away and grateful for this brother's willingness to love me in such a concrete way. I am grateful for the Adams and my Strong Tower family for loving me so well over the years.

Lastly, I want to thank the Brown family for literally being my homies, friends, and second family! Words won't do any justice to what they have been to me for so many years. I have known this family for 13 years, and I cannot imagine life without them. I met Zo on the campus of Tuskegee University as a freshman. With my abusive background with men, Zo was definitely different than any other man I encountered as a 17 year old. Most of the men I came in contact with were either abusive or out to get something from me, but Zo's genuine personality and love for God drew me to him. He was extremely gentle and kind, and he checked on me all the time after I became a new believer my first year of college. I remember telling him, "You're like the dad I wish I had." Zo and A. Brown have stayed in contact with me consistently over the years, and we have always stayed connected. When I went to an inner-city ministry as a 20 year old, Zo was working there. When I decided to join Strong Tower, Zo was the assistant pastor. I fell in love with this family and their beautiful children. I had the privilege of teaching their son for a year and a half at Valiant Cross Academy.

There have been countless phone calls, texts, and life on life that have taken place over the years. I lived with the Browns for a year before I purchased my own home, and it was indeed a blessing! My life is an open book before them, and it's hard to stay away from them for an entire week! A week feels way too long because of the genuine connection we have. They have seen my prosper, and they have seen me flat on my face, yet they have loved me through it. If the Lord allows me to have a family, you better believe this family will be a part of my family. Their prayers, laughs, rebukes, and encouragement pushed me to Jesus in ways that I will never forget. When I didn't have the strength to fight, they fought with me and for me. When I wanted to throw in the towel and walk away from God, their prayers held me together. They have been the hands and feet of Jesus in my life, and I couldn't ask for better friends. They have shown up in my life day in and day out, and I would not be the woman I am today without them.

The most loving thing Zo has told me hurt deeply, but it opened my eyes very quickly, "You need to repent and turn to Jesus. Turn the other way Quani. If you continue on this way, you will hurt so many people who love you." It was hard hearing that from a man you love like a dad. What hurt worse was he was right. I was so angry with the Lord for not giving me a husband and saddened by my experiences with men that I was in complete rebellion. I decided to give women or one woman a try emotionally not knowing the dire consequences. When I was in that stage, Zo held my hand through it and I came out on the right side. I decided to say no to my flesh and yes to the cross. When I think of the Browns and all of my family at Strong Tower, I think of this verse, "I thank my God upon every remembrance of you" (*King James Version*, Philippians 1:3).

TRUSTING GOD/ DATING

Some of the hardest trials I have had to face and walk through have been in the area of dating. As I write this chapter, a part of me is ashamed, embarrassed, and contemplating whether or not I should lay it on out there. However, the Lord has come to set the captives free, and He has finally given me freedom in this area of my life. I am no longer ashamed of what I have done, but I do hope to encourage the feeble hearts of single women who feel broken beyond repair. Let me start from the beginning. I believe every symptom has its roots, and they go deep. Before I talk about my dating history, I will first talk about my warped view of sex, women, and men. This goes back to the age of four.

My first encounter with a young man was extremely inappropriate, and even at the age of 4 or 5, I was aware of the wrongdoing. When my brother's friend asked to touch me in between my legs, I knew he wasn't supposed to touch me in that area. However, out of fear, I gave in and gained a core belief that day: "Men like what girls have in the middle." In other words, I figured out quickly that sex was a way to get the attention and shallow affection of a man. Most of my damaging encounters with men came in the form of compliments and touches. Since my father was absent during my younger years, I yearned for my attention and affection. I was extremely naive, and many older boys took complete advantage of that. I remember carrying deep shame at the age of five and adopting the belief that I was a "hoe" because men couldn't keep their hands off of me.

I liked boys and had several crushes; however, Satan presented the opportunity to watch porn and experiment with a young lady. I remember the showing of body parts, dry humping, and playing with objects. My mind had been tainted by my first experience, and I didn't talk to an adult about these feelings. The desire to be wanted, loved, and cared for only intensified as I got older. The affirmation, acceptance, and love that every child longs for was left empty due to my parents lack thereof. Although my grandmother filled that void as a parent, my heart had already been damaged and left with a gaping hole that I longed for my parents to fill. I wanted to hear: "You're beautiful!" "You are enough no matter what the world says!" Nonetheless, I received disappointment after disappointment. Rejection after rejection from parents whom I still loved so deeply. Although God has restored those relationships, the damage had already been done. I can vividly remember fantasizing about my future life: "A beautiful child with no father around to take care of him or her." That was my dream as a young girl.

I am a firm believer in this saying, "Children will more than likely repeat or live out what they see." Now, let me clarify something: I have not repeated every mistake or behavior of my parents. By the grace of God, I look like my mother, but God has spared me from having any children out of wedlock and I have never been physically abused by a man. Nevertheless, the relationship patterns I have repeated point to a core belief and behavior I have witnessed firsthand. Since men have mentioned how cute I was and liked my shape, I believed physical beauty and sex were the keys to keeping a man's attention. My mother has always had a nice shape and over the years, I have seen so many men approach her simply because of her curves. They have gawked over her assets and attention and affection were freely given as a result. With those same assets (hips and all), I learned to hiddenly flaunt my figure. I knew I was shapely and what fit right so capturing the eyes of a man wasn't hard for me. Ironically, I grew tired of men only wanting me because I was shapely, and I became fearful of them.

My sexual fantasies were all in my head, and my back up plan was to be with a woman if loving a man didn't work out. My first sexual encounter came at 14 when I was frustrated with hearing my friends talk about their sexual encounters, so I decided to "get some." The first time I had sex I remember being emotionless. He was 7 years older, and I just wanted to experience "it." Sadly, as we laid together, this was the only thought that popped in my head, "He's wasting his time, and this is probably the only man who will ever want me." The self-hatred was real! I was so distraught over how my parents treated me and internalized the sexual abuse to the point that I believed I was worthless. I felt discarded, dirty, and not worthwhile, and most men found it easy to take advantage of that. I have been intimate with four men over the course of 30 years. I started having sex at 14, and I stopped at 16. Eventually, I started to become self aware and uneasy about my choices. After each encounter, I felt used and that feeling was unbearable. I contracted two curable sexually transmitted diseases, and I didn't want to keep giving my body away just to be hurt again.

Looking back on that time, I see how God used a friend from Brooklyn to open my eyes to my foolish behavior. One day like many before that, I went to church with her. Her pastor preached on the consequences of sexual intercourse outside of marriage, and it frightened me deeply. He said the sexually immoral person would spend eternity in hell, and I believed him! I was terrified of dying and going to hell, so I made a commitment to wait until I was married to have sex. Lastly, I wanted to wait for a man that really loved me if he existed, so I became completely celibate. I have stuck to that commitment; however, my naivety and the desire to be loved has produced its share of heartache and pain. Let's start with the first guy I dated after I began working for C.G.M.

This guy was actually from Africa, South Africa that is. How we met was strange and interesting to say the least. He heard about C.G.M. through Sho Baraka. Sho Baraka, a christian hip-hop artist, was doing a concert in South Africa, and he happened to be there. How crazy is that! He emailed the ministry, and A. Conley, my best friend and coworker, received the email. She sent the email to me since I worked directly with people who desired to be a part of the summer internship. We emailed back and forth and spoke on the phone once, and I received a Facebook request from him. I accepted it, and he made his intentions known through comments and eventually, we exchanged numbers.

If I am honest, he wasn't my type, but I liked the attention he was giving me. He was okay looking to me, so I said yes to getting to know him. I loved our conversations, and he seemed very mature and the Lord was always on his lips. He was about 12 years older than me, so his life experience surpassed mine.

He was honest about his previous marriage in which his wife was unfaithful. I inquired about the validity of this through one of his friends, and his story was accurate. He was a nice guy, but he didn't like the idea of my pastors being so involved from the beginning. He eventually fell on hard times and asked me to send him money, and I refused. My pastors saw a lot of red flags, and they didn't believe he was the one for me. After months of conversing and skyping, I had to make a decision. With the disapproval of my pastors and others, I really wanted to hear from the Lord on this matter. As He always does, God spoke clearly through a brother and friend E. Armster and Proverbs 1: "Wisdom shouts in the street, she lifts her voice in the square; at the head of the noisy *streets*, she cries out; at the entrance of the gates in the city she utters her sayings: "How long, O naive ones, will you love being simple-minded? And scoffers delight themselves in scoffing and fools hate knowledge? Turn to reproof, Behold, I will pour out my spirit on you; I will make my words known to you. Because I called and you refused, I stretched out my hand and no one paid attention; And you neglected all my counsel and did not want my reproof; I will also laugh at your calamity (*Updated New American Standard*, Proverbs 1:20-26).

The Lord had been speaking for some time now. He spoke

clearly through my pastor and other friends. He spoke through the nudging of the Holy Spirit, and he confirmed it through His word. His wisdom was crying out to me, and if I didn't listen, calamity would soon be my fate. A conversation with my brother led me to this scripture. E. Armster approached me at church one day, and he asked me about "my friend." I told him that I wasn't sure of what to do. My heart was already in Africa because the thought of being loved captivated me. He asked me if I ever read Proverbs 1, and my response was, "Of course! That is my favorite scripture. I use that scripture with the children at C.G.M. all the time." It was in that moment that conviction ripped through my entire body.

I left the church that day, sat on my couch, and read Proverbs 1, and I knew I had to end the relationship. God spoke so clear that I couldn't deny His voice. I emailed "my friend" and told him that I could no longer continue in this relationship, and I never looked back. That situation taught me a valuable lesson about godly counsel. God will speak through multiple sources to get the attention of His beloved.

There was another guy, before I met the guy who I can honestly say I loved. The guy before "him" was a christian rapper who liked me for some time, and I honestly wasn't interested whatsoever. He was younger than me by three or four years, and he simply wasn't my type. Honestly, every man I've dated looks different, but each one has a look or personality that intrigues me. Anyway, after breaking it off with the guy in Africa, my mind started to give "the christian rapper" a thought. He was young, but he was a believer. He was attractive, but not initially my go to. At that particular time in my life, I was 24 or 25. I dated the guy in Africa around the age of 23 or 24. This particular guy was three years younger, but he was cool. I decided to inbox and invite him to Mic Check (an open mic night). Prior to that, I had conversations about him with some of my friends and brothers, and they thought I was being too picky because I was ignoring his advances. So, I decided to see how he would respond to an invite to Mic Check. He readily accepted the invite, and we began talking on the phone. He expressed his interest again, and I was happy he did. If I am honest, he filled a void that existed after I broke it off with the previous guy. Once I got a taste of the dating world at 23/24, I liked the attention and comfort it gave me. Sadly, it has cost me many restless nights, heartbreak after heartbreak, and deep anger towards men.

He and I began talking on the phone frequently. I came to one of his shows, and he offered to take me out on a date and give me a gift. I was ecstatic because he was a really nice guy, and our conversations were centered on prayer and the Lord. However, I noticed he had a girlfriend prior to talking to me, so I went on her page just to read the comments under her pictures. She was indeed attractive, and I wondered if he still had feelings for her. I saw recent comments from him, and I was devastated. The date and gift he promised never happened, and I backed away completely. It hurt deeply because it confused me. He literally liked me two years prior to me even giving it a second thought. He showered me with compliments, and he was clear that he was interested. I was disappointed again, and several months later, I received a phone call from him. I was shocked and knew I wasn't going to be the one reaching out. He apologized and asked for my forgiveness, and we decided to treat each other as friends and brothers and sisters in the Lord. That was the most genuine and heartfelt apology I have ever received from a man before "he" came into the picture.

It's weird to talk about "him" because he is someone that I know loved me genuinely. The amount of love and respect we have for one another is real, yet attraction gets in the way of that. If I can be honest, I wish "he" could be my knight and shining armour. The one who God made to love Chaquana, but the standards and non-negotiables that are a top priority for me were missing. It blows my mind how someone can love you so deeply, yet miss the main ingredients that make a relationship last. The heart of this man is precious, but there are parts of him that brought on some of the deepest pain that I ever experienced. I remember being balled up in closet crying my eyes out after he hurt again. It's like opening up your heart again only for your heart to be stomped on. Although there are no hard feelings toward him, close friendship is not possible because of the emotional intimacy that was shared. We never touched or kissed. He gave me a peck on the lips once; however, our relationship was never physical. It is because of that reason that our bond is so tight. This relationship had the most ups and downs, yet the feelings of unforgiveness and anger have completely dissipated.

I met him when he was 17, and I was 20. There was no interest at that time; however, I thought he was attractive. When I would see him, I would get some butterflies in my stomach, but I brushed it off as mere attraction. Several years later, we ran into each at a lake house when I led the C.G.M. interns in 2015. I knew from the time I stepped out of that van, he was attracted to me. I could sense his gaze and admiration from afar. We knew each other because we had met several years prior to that. He sat near me, and he asked me was I married and we talked about singleness. He went wherever I went, and I knew he was interested. You know the funny thing about this story: "I knew from looking at him that he was immature and not ready to give me the maturity I needed." The Lord spoke some time after that and told me directly from the scriptures that he was not the one. I remember where I was sitting, what city I was in, and the scripture he gave me, yet I was hoping God got it wrong this time. My pastors warned me again and encouraged me in my fight to stay away from him. However, he came in and out of my life and each time I gave in. He and I dated off and on since 2015. There were times when we didn't talk to one another, and there were times when we were just friends.

Recently, he came back into my life after a terrible and traumatic dating experience that I will discuss later on. He was there; I knew he cared and still loved me. The same attraction was there, but it seemed to get stronger the more we connected and talked through things. I had to make a decision. Although he is one of the sweetest and most respectful men I have ever encountered, spiritually I know for sure he is not where he needs to be to pursue a godly woman. Our conversations rarely touch on the topic of Jesus unless I bring it up. He doesn't believe the Bible is 100% true, and the reading of the scriptures in his life is little to none unless I encourage it. He faithfully goes to church, and he is in constant fellowship with other believers; however, deep intimacy with God seems to be lacking. Discipleship, sharing his faith, and being on mission for God is not on his radar, and it hasn't been since I met him. Financially, he struggles and dates were few. As I write this, it hurts reading what I am actually putting on paper. Let me tell you why it hurts. Jesus is the best thing that has ever happened to me. He is the hope of my today, tomorrow, and my forever with Him. How can I say I love God, yet give my heart away to a man who doesn't make Jesus his everything? As cute and great as "he" is, if "he" is not sincerely plugged into Jesus, our relationship won't last. Jesus has to be the foundation not how we "feel" about each other because feelings fade. I had to learn to really trust God with this particular guy and ask Him to help me say no to the temptation of going back to someone who is clearly "not the one."

After "he" and I called it quits for the uptenth time, two months later I met "Q dawg." My best friend told me about "POF" or "Plenty of Fish." I created a profile a while back, but I decided to add some cute pictures to see if I could get some quality interest. Shortly after I changed up my pictures, I received several inboxes. Many of the men I ignored or simply and kindly declined their advances.

One evening while in bed, I got an inbox from a gentlemen who I thought was cute. I liked the conversation, so I showed my pastor who he was, and he knew him! My pastor said he seemed like a nice guy, so I decided to go on a date. We went to Lek's Railroad Thai, and we really had a great time. The conversation was nice, and afterwards, we went to the bookstore and had coffee!! As a nerd, avid reader, and teacher, the bookstore is like Disney World to me. We talked about my favorite book "The Autobiography of Malcolm X" amongst other things, so I was so happy! Before that took place, I created a vision board and put the things I was looking forward to for the new year, and a good man was one of them! I was blindsided and ready to move on from "him."

I told my pastors about him, and T. wanted to speak to him right from the beginning. I told "Q dawg" about my pastors and numbers were exchanged. My pastors saw me go through the pain of dating before, so they wanted to protect me from another cycle of disappointment. "Q dawg" was married previously, and he stated that his marriage didn't work because they couldn't get along. We frequently talked about the word and the Lord; however, I wasn't sure of a true conversion to Christ. Church attendance and submission to authority are top priorities on my list, yet his church attendance was limited.

We talked about marriage, and he even asked me to send him pictures of the engagement ring I wanted. He dated me every week, and the affection and connection were amazing! I loved the walks downtown, and when I was with him, I felt like the only woman in the room. His focus and attention were on me. However, there were some compromises I made that I was convicted of. We started kissing and touching. We decided to back away from kissing and then we would fall back into it. Honestly, my love language is physical touch, so I had to really ask the Lord for help in that area because the kisses were sweet and his affection made me feel safe. After a while, I started to feel convicted, so I decided to fast and pray and the Lord gave me this scripture: "Flee immorality. Every other sin that a man commits is outside the body, but the immoral man sins against his own body. Or do you not know that your body is a temple of the Holy Spirit who is in you, whom you have from God, and that you are not your own? For you have been bought with a price: therefore glorify God in your body" (*Updated New American Standard,* 1 Corinthians 6:18-20).

Above all else, I wanted to honor God with my body and I wanted His will to be done, so I fasted and sought Him for seven days, and my answer came during that week. I started to feel convicted and concerned about "Q dawgs" commitment to the local body of believers. Whenever I would discuss my pastors or the importance of community, he expressed his concern or disapproval of the intentionality and involvement of my community/ pastors. Let me make something very clear. My pastors are my shepherds. They have been given the authority to shepherd my soul as their church member and sister in the Lord. As a single woman, they are my covering along with the Lord. If my covering is not okay with my dating choices and their concerns line up with scripture, I am obliged to obey them! The Bible is clear about the role of a shepherd: "Obey your leaders and submit to them, for they are keeping watch over your souls as those who will have to give an account. Let them do this with joy and not with groaning, for that would be of no advantage to you" (*English Standard Version*, Hebrews 13:17).

My pastors were not fond of his choice to avoid a real conversation with them, and their concerns were legitimate. I knew if I continued ignoring and dismissing their concerns, I would be with a man who didn't take church authority and submission seriously. If I were to get married to him and things got hard, who would we turn to if he didn't believe in biblical submission to church authority? At the end of the day, the body of Christ has my back until I said "I do." The week of my fast I had a very detailed dream. I knew this dream was from the Lord because when I woke up I felt concerned, and I remembered every detail of the dream. In this dream, a woman came to me and told me she knew "Q dawg." She told me that he came into her life and suddenly disappeared, and I knew from that conversation that he would do the same to me. Moreover, the woman in the dream seemed very familiar. Before the dream, he and I had an amazing date night, and it was hard not to enjoy the company of this sweet man. His charm was hard to resist. I posted several pictures on my instagram account, but I decided to post one to Facebook. He saw me put the picture up, and he was okay with it. Nonetheless, I decided to tag him in the picture since we were openly dating anyway. I had just gotten off the phone with him, and I could tell from my notifications that he removed the tag. I was confused and hurt, so I decided to ask about it.

He told me that he didn't want people to be in his business and that I should have asked. I was confused because he watched me put the picture up after we discussed engagement rings. We were supposed to go on a date that week, and he stopped responding to me. I knew something was off by his silence. I ran into him at the gym, and he was distant and cold. He said he wasn't ignoring me, and he asked me to remove the picture. I removed the picture, and he communicated that he wasn't in the mood to talk about anything. I gave him his space, and I told my roommate about the dream I had after I posted the picture. My roommate looked at me and said, "Somebody came to me about the picture you posted. She asked me if you knew anything about his past, and I told her I wasn't sure. I told her to come to you." My response was, "I had a dream somebody was going to come to me. This is crazy. God gave me that dream for a reason." My only and last questions was this: "Do I know her?" My roommate responded with a clear yes and stated that she had been in my home. I was so hurt and disappointed.

The young woman, friend, and sister in Christ called me and told me she knew "Q dawg" and that his character and actions were skeptical and concerning. She went so far as to say these alarming and eye opening words: "If you were to invite me to your wedding, and he was the groom, I wouldn't go." I needed to hear that. He was upset about a picture; he was clearly hiding something, and he was ignoring me. After I ran into him at the gym, I didn't hear from him for two months. I tried to see what I did wrong, and it didn't make sense to me that a grown man over 40 couldn't communicate what was wrong. I knew he was hiding something, and I didn't like feeling discarded and mistreated for something I was bewildered about. I knew that was God's way of telling me he wasn't the one and to move on.

I got a text after two months, and I politely told him "I have moved on." He asked for an apology for how he was treated which concerned me because I never mistreated him. Shortly after that I ran into him, he said that he didn't like people in his business and my pastors in our business was a concern for him. I politely listened and told him it was nice seeing him. I knew that was the end of any connection we had, and I was completely okay with that based on his actions.

Two months later, "Light skin" came into the picture. The pattern I am painting should be clear by now. Each time I broke it off with a guy, I didn't give myself time to heal or recuperate. I was on to the next two or three months later. I was eager to date and find "the one" not realizing that Jesus was the one I was really trying to get to. Sadly, it took multiple experiences and this one in particular to wake me up from my slumber. From 23/24 to 29/30, I have made poor choices in my selection of men out of naivety, fear of loneliness, discontentment, and a genuine desire to be loved and cared for.

This last guy was the push I needed to take a step back and evaluate my choices. I have seen fine men on television and in passing, but this man was absolutely gorgeous! He was my type from top to bottom, and I honestly believed he would be different. Nevertheless, the enemy knows our weaknesses, and he knows Chaquana's kryptonite is men. Recently, I was on Facebook, and I played a game that said this of my personality: "Chaquana is the ultimate true friend. Chaquana sticks by you through it all. Babies, teens, adults, and old folks adore her. Although she's an amazing "greatest friend ever" kind of woman, she's also incredibly sexy and alluring. Many men have been driven crazy from their addiction to her. And that is her only down side. When you're not with Chaquana, life just doesn't seem quite as good."

My down side has been my relationships with the opposite sex, and I have suffered tremendously in this area. The last guy was a surprise to me. I didn't see it coming, and I didn't see the pain that was coming my way shortly after. I had just gotten back from a beach trip with some friends, and I got a friend request from a guy who looked familiar. I saw him at Strong Tower a couple of years ago, but I was not interested and involved with "him" at the time. I knew when he added me that an inbox would come shortly there after.

Due to my constant interactions with men, I know when an interest arises. I am a good reader of body language and natural attraction. I have encountered men in my day to day routine who show interest, and it doesn't take me by surprise. Shortly thereafter, he messaged me and expressed interest. He wants to be friends and get to know me because he was impressed by my career choice and interest. We exchanged numbers, and things began to circulate from there. My pastors knew him among other brothers, and they liked him. I visited him in South Carolina, and he visited me in Montgomery. Things moved quickly, and we began dating shortly after.

I decided to fast and pray and felt God giving me a yes to go forward with the relationship. We read the word together, stay on the phone all night, and enjoy one another's company. I was quickly convinced this was from the Lord. I tell him that he needs to figure out if I am the one God has for him, so we don't waste each other's time. My pastors like him, and he meets my best friends in Memphis. Everybody is fond of him, and so am I until what is done in the dark comes to the light. When "light skin" approached me he admitted to having a son with a woman he dated off and on for 9 years. He told me about his struggle with pornography, masturbation, and women. He also told me that he was walking in obedience now and that his sexual sin was a thing of the past.

He respected my boundaries of waiting until marriage to have sex, but the time spent alone led to touching and kissing. There were times when that didn't happen at all, but I quickly came to see that he lacked self-control in that area. I would give in out of a desire to please and a desire to be intimate. We were both wrong, and I started to be convicted once again in this area. I remember telling him that I didn't want to touch because it displeased the Lord. We repented, cried, and backed away from it. His words and questions often went to sexual matters, and he seemed mesmerized by me. I am not innocent at all because I engaged in the conversations and made sure I looked attractive around him to keep his attention. We enjoyed several and consistent dates, trips, and time well-spent until he confessed his truth. Before I get to that truth, I picked up on something that concerned me: his lack of self-control and leadership, and his words about women. He was said, "If women threw it at me, I would take it." He then asked, "How do you feel about someone else coming into the "marriage bed?" I was shocked by his audacity and sexually saturated mind. Other things were said, and I cannot blame him for it because I allowed it.

One day in August, we attended the wedding of a young man I knew. It was at this wedding that he confessed to being unfaithful. He told me it happened in July after I left, and he was lonely. The young lady came on to him, and he gave in. He couldn't hold it in anymore, so he wanted to tell me. I later found out through my pastors that it happened twice, and he had done the same thing to the mother of his child several times. It hurt like hell, but I was still ready to love and forgive him if he got the help he needed. My heart started to drift away from him when I realized he knew what he was doing, yet he was unwilling to acknowledge his idolatry and sin.

I forgave him and continued to love him as a brother, but when I started to see that he didn't see the seriousness of his sin, I knew something was wrong. I gave him an ultimatum: Go back to South Carolina and get some help or get some help at Fisher's Farm in Montgomery. Fisher's Farm is an addiction program geared to help men make Christ their everything not their addiction. He didn't believe he had an issue that was an addiction. He admitted that since he had been a believer, he would go two to three months at a time without sexual intercourse and then fall back into it. Sex was his idol and not the almighty God, but he didn't believe it was. I knew I had to end it when we had a conversation about his habit. I told him that his sexual encounters were a lifestyle, and he had an addiction to sex. He looked me in my face and told me that he didn't have a problem, and he was victorious because he got back up every time he fell. My heart was deeply broken.

I remember bursting out in tears as I was driving one afternoon to attend a Zumba training. I remember fighting sadness, pain, and depression because I didn't understand why or how God could send me someone who couldn't stay faithful to me. I remember being completely embarrassed because I had to be honest with my pastor and closest friends about his problem. I knew I needed to end it, so I talked to my pastors again and they recommended I leave him alone. I blocked and deleted his number, blocked him on Facebook, and the things he left at my home were picked up. I deeply cared about him, but I knew God allowed this to happen to show me how committed and faithful he had been to me and will continue to be because he was my true husband.

One evening after he met with my pastors and it was clear that we needed to go our separate ways, I receive a missed call from him through an app we used to use to video chat. I missed his call and sent him a voicemail. I told him not to contact me and to trust the Lord with the process. At that point, I was heartbroken and I knew he needed serious help. Hope left me because he talked a good game spiritually and we even read the bible together, but his fruit did not match his words. When I decided to obey my shepherds and listen to God's leading, I knew I had to end the relationship. I heard God speak through the same scripture he used to speak to me about "him," but I ignored the voice of the Lord. I, once again, thought God had made a mistake. That same evening after I sent him that voicemail, I looked outside of my window and he was standing outside of my bedroom window looking at me. I screamed and ran out of my room to where my roommate was. I told her to quickly call the police and our pastors because I thought I saw "Light skin" outside the window.

We were both terrified at this point, so we hid in the hallway and waited on my pastor and the police to show up. My pastor drove around my home and didn't see anything. The police officer walked around and didn't see anything or anyone. I was confused, and I thought I was losing my mind. I saw a few missed calls from him, so I knew he found a way to contact me when he wasn't supposed to. Somehow, he figured out how to reach me even though his number was blocked. I unblocked his number to ask him if he was outside of the window. I called him several times, my pastor called him, and my roommate called him, but we received no answer. He finally picked up, and when I questioned him, he told me it wasn't him and that he had decided to go to Fisher's Farm to deal with his issues. He even went so far as to say, "Are you okay? Let me know if I need to come over there." My pastor was standing right next to me, and he knew dishonesty was coming from his lips. My naive self was still trying to believe it wasn't so!

Eventually, he confessed to my pastor because he was embarrassed that I responded in such a way. According to him, he had no intentions of scaring or harming me; he simply missed me. That night, my roommates and I spent the night at my pastor's house where I tossed and turned all night. I was embarrassed, hurt, and ashamed that I had attracted such an unstable man, and my pastor, his wife, and my roommates had to witness it. My nights after that were hard, and I remember trying to keep my cries low, so my roommates couldn't hear me weep. Another broken heart, another disappointment, and I was the blame. I became extremely depressed, suicidal, and heavy. I had to be an excellent teacher while battling depression. I had to consider pure joy when I didn't believe Jesus was enough to give me everything I need. I contemplated not going to church and spending some time being angry with God since He disappointed me once again.

Then God showed up! I decided to keep going to church and one morning, Sunday school blessed me. We were talking about trials and suffering, and Zo and F. Turner dropped some nuggets. Zo mentioned the story of Joseph, and he stated that God knew

Joseph was alive and would use him to help his brothers who had done evil to him. He went on to say that God could tell us why things happen, but he uses it to bring about His purpose for His glory. I knew that God wanted Chaquana to see that a mere human being wasn't capable of loving me the way I always desired to be loved. He was the only one that can and will fill the void of loneliness, disappointment, and shame. Every time I fell on my face, he was there. Every time I asked him to show me if I should continue in this relationship or that relationship, he made it clear that He was the most faithful, loving, and consistent God. It finally hit me that Jesus is truly the most solid and loving being that loves me recklessly because He has protected me from every single man that wasn't for me! I received some battle wounds, but I came out stronger and wiser than before.

A dear brother stated that sometimes God allows people in the body of Christ to go through things to show others what perseverance looks like. During that difficult time, K. Adams and I became close. He knew about my depression, deep sadness, and suicidal ideations. That brother called to check on me consistently, texted me, and prayed me through my last semester at Valiant Cross. The break up with "Light skin," and the desire to perform was killing me emotionally and spiritually to the point of praying for the desire not to just end it all. I was just tired, but the prayers of God's people, His word, and the local church encouraged me to keep fighting the good fight of faith. The days following that got easier. The Lord literally gave me strength, joy, and peace like a river!! I can't explain how I made it out of that dark place, but what I can say is, "I knew the Lord wanted me to be free from using things and people as a source of comfort and run to Him." I started to go to counseling and work through the hurt and betrayal. I ran to the Lord when I was lonely and confessed my sin and shortcomings. Six months later, I can say confidently that I am okay. Some days I feels the hurt and pain, and many days I don't. Men have come into the picture after "Light skin" and by the grace of God, I said no. "He" came back into the picture and feelings started to arise, and I had to cut it off completely. I am okay and excited about my journey with the Lord because His love is so much sweeter after the trial.

During those nights of hidden cries and suicidal thoughts, I felt the love of Jesus. He was right there with me, encouraging me through His word and precious Holy Spirit. He gave me a greater desire to know, love, and serve Him, and I finally feel whole. Even though marriage is still a desire, I am okay if Jesus is the only husband I get to experience on this side of heaven because He has been the sweetest husband I've known. When I desire companionship, I run to Him and the amazing friends He has given me. God has shown me how faithful and kind He is, and now I can consider it pure joy when I face trials because I know who is facing the trial with me! He is! He is my rock, my safe place, my strong tower, and my help! I know He loves me, and I am convinced that He is jealous for Chaquana Monique Muhammad Townsend. I am a jewel and a King has to be able to handle a jewel. He is my rescuer and protector, and I am grateful for Him.

Single ladies, I know it is hard to believe that God has not forgotten you. I know it is hard to believe that He cares when you see people getting engaged, married, and pregnant right in front of your face. He is the God who sees, who knows, and who cares. He does not withhold any good thing from those who walk uprightly (*New American Standard,* Psalm 84:11). He wants you to believe and know that true contentment comes from Him and Him alone. The joy I feel is unreal! I am smiling more than I ever smiled, and I am so excited about working for the kingdom of God because Jesus is finally enough. His love has overtaken me! I am not pregnant! Thank you Lord! I am not suffering from a sexually transmitted disease. I am not in an unhappy relationship. I am whole and complete because I finally see who was there the whole time. If He did it for me, He can do it for you! I am living my dreams by teaching at a school I adore despite the fights and crooked system. I am publishing my first book and starting a business soon! God is faithful! I have always dreamed of being a writer and owning a business that empowers women. He is doing it because when I am doing His will, joy follows. Pursue Him and He will give you the desires of your heart (*New International Version,* Psalm 37:4).

Lastly, I want to acknowledge a woman who is indeed one of the biggest advocates, supporters, and best friends I could ask for. Kellee Ferguson is probably the only single woman that I have met with the healthiest and most honest approach to dating. She has taught me to love myself over the years. She has laughed at me when I did silly things and rebuked and encouraged me when I needed to hear hard truth. Most importantly, she has taught me many valuable lessons as a single woman. She has encouraged me to never settle! If that man does not have the non-negotiables you need and desire, leave him alone! She never judged me or belittled my feelings. She honestly and lovingly told me to own my truth.

I honestly don't know where I would be without such a solid and real friendship. I can be completely vulnerable and honest with her even when it hurts. She knows me very well and will call me out my dishonesty. She knows when I am hurting, and she knows when I am free. She is a woman that I admire for her courage, hard work, and willingness to go after what she wants. Her confidence and assurance in her beauty is convicting and encouraging. Thank you Kellee for helping me to see the beauty and strength I didn't know I had. You love me beyond my flaws, and I love being your friend and travel buddy. I know love is possible because you are a living example of what it means to never settle for less. I love you, and thank you for being my rock on earth during the good and the bad.

SUICIDE/HOPE

One of my biggest temptations on this side of heaven is the desire to "leave this earth" when life is overwhelming. The Lord's faithfulness has been an anchor for my soul, but there were several instances as a believer that I had completely lost hope. Most times the suicidal ideations came from shame, embarrassment, rejection, and deep fear. These times in my life I made a mistake and didn't believe I could be loved or cleansed from it. The notion or idea of suicide pushes a person to believe that God's truth, comfort, and love aren't enough in that moment. Life has its challenges and many ups and downs accompany it; however, the grace, love, and compassion of Jesus can help us in any situation. I am reminded of God's rescuing power in the book of Psalms. When we turn to God in the midst of our pain, He is a deliverer and healer:

> "I sought the Lord, and he answered me;
> he delivered me from all my fears.
> Those who look to him are radiant;
> their faces are never covered with shame.
> This poor man called, and the Lord heard him;
> he saved him out of all his troubles.
> The angel of the Lord encamps around those who fear him,
> and he delivers them (*New International Version*, Psalm 34).

In times of difficulty, especially in the case of suicide, we must seek the Lord and surround ourselves with people who love us and care about our well-being. Isolation should never be the go to when you are struggling emotionally. Our thoughts can lead us down paths that we should never travel. When I am struggling, I have had to learn to go spend the night with some friends. Being around others and confessing your struggles, protects you from yourself. When the truth is out, there is freedom and your brothers and sisters can pray for your healing: "Therefore confess your sins to each other and pray for each other so that you may be healed. The prayer of a righteous person is powerful and effective (*New International Version,* James 5:16).

There is something that happens when the people of God get together and pray! I can vividly remember going through difficult seasons and feeling the prayers of the righteous giving me the strength to go on. I knew there was no way I would have made it without dear brothers and sisters praying and fasting for me. My dear brother and sister, you are not alone in your struggle with depression, suicide, and hopelessness. Seek Him, counseling, and community and watch the days get a little easier. God promises to make all things new on the day of completion:

"Being confident of this, that he who began a good work in you will carry it on to completion until the day of Christ Jesus" (*New International Version*, Philippians 1:6).

ABOUT THE AUTHOR

Chaquana Monique Muhammad Townsend was born in Bronx, New York on October 15, 1988. She is the daughter of Linda Townsend and Abdus Ali (Robert Napper). She has three siblings on her mother's side, David, Benjamin, and Csniqua and 18 or more siblings on her father's side. Chaquana was raised by her grandmother from the time she was four until the age of thirteen in New Orleans, Louisiana. Her roots stem from both New York and New Orleans culture.

She moved back to New York at thirteen years of age and finished high school while there. The neglect of her parents, past abuse and disappointment, the death of her grandmother, and the fear of repeated a vicious cycle pushed Chaquana to pursue college at Tuskegee University. It was there that she found the hope of the gospel that completely and radically changed her life and perspective. After college, she pursued a Master's in Christian Counseling where she faced the pain and reality of her abuse and began the process of deep healing. She eventually moved to Montgomery where she worked for Common Ground Montgomery and joined Strong Tower at Washington Park. She currently lives in Washington Park and teaches 8th grade English at Southlawn Middle School. She dreams of one day owning her own business where she can use teaching, dance, ministry, and writing to glorify God. She is currently a member of Flatline Church at Chisolm, and she is an ESL teacher, dancer, and writer.

TO THE LOVER
OF MY SOUL

Words cannot describe what you mean to me. You are the one true husband and lover I have been waiting for my entire life! Thank you for choosing me before the foundation of the world to be yours and yours alone. Thank you for knowing me deeply and still sticking by my side. Your love is like no other. It holds me together when life is falling apart. It keeps me going when it makes more sense to give up. You have loved me with an indescribable love. A love that convicts. A love that encourages, and a love that has changed my entire being. Jesus, I am so grateful for a God who never fails!

This journey with you has been joyous, painful, exciting, scary, and life-giving. You have given me strength and courage that I did not have. You have rescued me from people and situations that were damaging to my soul. I want to love you forever and live to make you known. I pray that my nieces and nephews get to taste the goodness of your love. I pray that my sister, mother, father, and extended family members get to see the goodness of the Lord in the land of the living. Your love overflows and grips every part of my soul. Thank you for being mine, and I pray that my heart falls deeper and deeper in love with you. Lord, keep my eyes stayed on you. Hold me when I feel alone and the enemy tries to tell me lies. I love you Lord. Thank you for hearing my cries. May my legacy and impact be a reflection of what you have done and the power of the cross. My life belongs to you. I look forward to worshipping you forever!

DEAR BLACK MAN

When I think of you, I think of hope. I think of beauty in its purest form. I am so sorry that society sees you as an enemy. They have dehumanized you and torn apart your very essence. You are loved kings! You are amazing, and it is truly a privilege to know you. It is hard for many sisters to keep their eyes off such a beautiful sight. Sin has distorted God's plan for your life, but he is the master at perfecting what the world has disfigured. I will keep fighting for you and loving you even when your actions disappoint. You are still God's creation, made in His image for His glory, and I will treat you as such.

Black man, you are not a mistake or a menace to society. You are simply a product of a crooked and perverse world, and it is my prayer that you walk in the authority God has given you. Even though some of my experiences with you have been less than ideal, I refuse to label you as a curse because God made you uniquely. You are a gift to the world whether you believe it or not. God creates masterpiece kings, and I am sure you are a part of that greatness. So, I will pray for you, encourage you, and love on you every chance I get. You were made to shine. You were made to rule, and I pray that you one day you will see how amazing you truly are. May God protect you from the evil one and capture your heart with his love. Be kings!!!

DEAR BLACK WOMAN

Queens, you are the dopest beings on the face of the earth! Now, this is not a celebration of who's better because God made every race and ethnicity equally amazing; however, this is a celebration of the black woman-A woman who has endured so much, yet she still fights for joy and freedom when the world tries to trip her up. You are fierce! Beautiful is an understatement for the strength, courage, and divine essence you possess. You were made with a purpose, with a reason, and the world has always taken note of the black woman.

Sisters, let's use our giftings and beauty to reflect an amazing and glorious God. You are more than your hips, curves, and what God has given you to bless your mate if He so allows. You were made to point others to the goodness and magnificence of the creator, and I pray that you believe in the true beauty that He has given you. True beauty runs deeper than your outward appearance because it is a beauty that doesn't fade or run out. It is a quiet beauty that brings peace, satisfaction, joy, contentment, and depth to everyone around. It is a beauty that says no to evil but yes to God. Your beauty is undeniable, unshakable, and breathtaking because it came from an undeniable, unshakable, and breathtaking God. Be queens because God made you to rule!

DEAR SINGLE WOMEN

This book was birthed out of the pain of being single and hoping that the guy I was dating would be the one to numb the loneliness. I remember being on the phone with him after he confessed to being unfaithful telling him that I am going to start writing a book. This book was given life because the Lord knew He had a bigger purpose for my life, and it wasn't a ring from a man who couldn't stay faithful. Sis, I know what it feels like to believe something is wrong with you. I know what it feels like to live your entire life wanting to be loved, valued, and cared for only to receive disappointment after disappointment. I know what it feels like to be faithful to the Lord and still end up being alone. I know what it feels like to want something so bad and never get it.

Sisters, God has not forgotten about you because He is the only one who truly understands what it feels like to be alone. He was despised, rejected, and familiar with suffering. He was tempted just as we are, yet He was spotless because of who He is. He is the one who holds us together when we feel like giving up. He is the one who protects us when men come into the picture who are no good for us. He understands the lonely nights, the constant cries for help, and He will continue to meet us right where we are. Marriage is not the end all be all; Jesus is! God does not withhold any good thing from those who walk uprightly. He is good, and He is the one who gives us exactly what we need. His word stands true: "For your Maker is your husband-- the

LORD Almighty is his name-- the Holy One of Israel is your Redeemer; he is called the God of all the earth" (*New International Version,* Isaiah 54:5).

DEAR BLACK BOY
AND GIRL

You are our future hope and the leaders of tomorrow. Don't believe for one second that your life, opinion, and voice do not matter. You are a gift to your parents, teachers, family members, friends, and many others. Thank you for existing! Thank you for being you and allowing adults to take part in your amazing legacy. Cherish, respect, and love the adults around you who care for you more than you realize. You may not see it now, but their words of wisdom will make sense to you when you become an adult yourself. Use your influence and leadership to bring the world good and not harm.

We are rooting for you. It is you who make the world go round. It is you who give light to places that are dark. Your smile and life can bring joy to a place and a person because God created you to do such. I pray for the protection of your mind, heart, and soul. May God capture you with His love and keep you on the His path and not the path of the evil one. Shine Kings and Queens. Be great because the one who created you is great! You are truly a masterpiece and gift to a world that is looking for you to take center stage. The only way to continue to shine bright is to get your light from the one who shines brighter than anything else. He brings hope to the hopeless and light to the darkness. He is a father to the fatherless, and a husband to the one who is husbandless. Let Him be your guide because He will not lead you astray. May God keep you and help you to see that true love, acceptance, and hope come from Him. Be free, black boy and girl, to love a God that will never disappoint!

DEAR TEACHER/ LIFE CHANGER

I get it! I understand the sacrifice, time well spent, long days, and long nights. Brothers and sisters, your labor is NOT in vain. However, this letter has a flipside, and I really want you to listen: "Don't pour from an empty, overwhelmed, I just want to make others happy cup!" You are more than a teacher, and empty cups don't pour out. Those cups only get filled with more work, baggage, and weight. Let the Lord fill you help, so you are able to holistically, authentically, and righteously pour out! The battle is with the Lord, and your own heart, not with your students, parents, or administration. Give your students the filled up you, the content you, the you that believes in the help of a mighty God. Then, you teach with all your heart, mind, and soul!

Encourage your students/scholars to be themselves. Encourage them to be excellent because they were made by an excellent God. Encourage them to work hard rather than taking the easy way out and pray like crazy! Prayer will get you up in the morning and get you through the day. It will keep you teaching when you make up in your mind that teaching is for the birds. You are indeed a gift and life changer. Ask God to fill you with more of Him, so you can give His love to your students/scholars and those around. Lastly, don't neglect your own well-being or the well-being of your family. Your first mission is

your home and then it's your classroom. Believe it or not, character and education go hand in hand. I pray that your character and legacy reflect excellence and integrity which infiltrates your classroom. Teacher and life changer, I am praying
for you. I pray that God will fill you to the brim, so your light can spill over to them (your students/scholars). God bless you!

TO KELLEE, AVA, KASEY, AND HEATHER (MY BEST FRIENDS)

I cannot imagine life without you guys. I am completely floored and grateful for the opportunity to do life with such amazing queens! You guys have shown me what it looks like to love even when it's uncomfortable. Thank you for every year of friendship and every labor of love given and shown. I heard a quote that says, "You are the company you keep!" Well, based on my company, a sister is winning!! Every last one of you are absolutely amazing. You are amazing friends, girlfriends, fiances, and wives. You are a clear example and picture of God's loving kindness toward me, and I am forever indebted to you. I pray that God gives you the desires of your heart and blesses you tremendously. Thank you for being my sisters and friends for so many years!!!

I hope you feel loved and celebrated through this small token of Thanksgiving. I would not have made it out of many of my "situations" if I didn't have your prayers and sweet words of encouragement. If the Lord blesses me with a fine chocolate man, you better believe I will have every last one of you by my side! You are my gift and treasure on this side of heaven, and I love you as much as I love "mint chocolate chip ice cream." Thank you for rooting me on over the years, fighting with and for me, and telling me the truth even when it hurts. Your friendship means the world to me, and I pray that the Lord blesses us with many more years to come. Kellee, I love you so much, and this love is for life! Ava, you are my favorite light skinned sister! Kasey, you are my little bestie! Heather, you are the realest! I love all of you!

STUDY QUESTIONS FOR BELIEVERS, TEACHERS, AND STUDENTS

Please answer these questions honestly and ask the Lord to meet you right where you are. The scriptures are a guide and reference for you as you journey on to freedom in Christ.

Believers:

    How does your upbringing or past still affect you in the present?

    How have your parents, other family members, or friends wounded you?

    How do you think God views this tragedy or offense? How

would he want you to respond or deal with the pain of it? (Romans 8; Genesis 50; John 16; Psalm 147:3)

What does God do for those who mourn or deal with pain? (Psalm 147:3; Matthew 5:4; Psalm 34:18; Isaiah 53:4-6)

Are you carrying any undealt with unforgiveness? What does the bible say about
forgiveness? (Mark 11:25; Matthew 6:14-15; Ephesians 4: 26-27; Ephesians 4:32)

Are there any idols in your life that you need to confess to God? What does God say about confession? (Exodus 20:3-5; James 5:16; 1 John 1:9; Proverbs 28:13; Psalm 32:5)

TEACHERS

What is the why behind your job? In other words, why do you teach?

Are you glorifying God in every aspect of your teaching? How so? What does God say about work? (Colossians 3:23; Psalm 90:17; Proverbs 12:11; Proverbs 13:4)

Do you pray for your students, their parents, your coworkers, and your own mental stability? What does God say about prayer? (1 John 5:14-15; 1 Chronicles 16:8-12; 2 Chronicles 7:14; Ephesians 6:18)

Has teaching become your idol or god? Are you setting realistic boundaries with work? (Exodus 20:3-12)

How do you view "your job?" Are you still fulfilling the

"Great Commission?" What is the "Great Commission?" (Matthew 28:16-20)

How are you loving on your students? How are you building them up with your words rather than tearing them down? (Ephesians 4:29-32)

When you fall or mess up, are you quick to ask for forgiveness, confess your sins, and share your struggle with others? Why or why not?

What does God's grace look like for you at your job? What is grace? (2 Corinthians 12:8-9; Romans 3:20-24; John 1:14)

STUDENTS

How are you honoring God with your school work? What does it mean to honor God with your school work? (1 Corinthians 10:31; 1 Corinthians 6:20; Proverbs 3:9)

Who are your friends? Are your friends a good influence or bad influence on you? What does God say about the company you keep? (1 Corinthians 15:33; 2 Corinthians 6:14; Proverbs 13:20; Proverbs 14:7)

How are you respecting your teachers and other school authorities? What does the bible say about respect? Why should we respect those in authority? (Romans 13:1-7; Matthew 7:12; Romans 12; Philippians 2)

How are you honoring and obeying your parents' authority? What does the bible say about obeying your parents? (Ephesians 6:1-9)

STUDY QUESTIONS AND SCRIPTURES FOR PERSONAL GROWTH

Marriage, Singleness, Sex, Suicide, Community, and Freedom.

What does God say about singleness? What does God say about marriage? How should we view each season of life? (1 Corinthians 7:1-40; Genesis 2:18; Genesis 2:22-24; Proverbs 12:4; Proverbs 18:22; Ephesians 5:22-33)

How do you view your singleness? Is it a gift or a curse? Where did this thinking come from? How have you surrendered your viewpoint to the Lord?

How do you view your marriage or future marriage? What does it look like to honor God as a wife based on the scriptures above?

What does the bible say about sex? As a single woman, how

are you fleeing from sexual immorality? (Ephesians 5:33; Genesis 2:24; Hebrews 13:4; 1 Corinthians 6:12-20)

What does the bible say about sex for the married person? Are there any restrictions with sex in marriage? (1 Corinthians 6:12-10; 1 Corinthians 7; Matthew 5:28; 1 Thessalonians 4:3-5)

Does the bible speak to suicide? If you are struggling emotionally, how does God speak to your situation? Is there hope for the weary and heavy laden according to the bible? (Matthew 11:28-30; Psalm 34; Psalm 23)

Is community important to God? Is community important to you? What does God say about the body of Christ and the fellowship of the saints? (1 Corinthians 12:12-31; Romans 12:4-5; Ephesians 4:4; Hebrews 10:25)

What does the bible say about freedom? What does freedom look like for the believer? (Galatians 5:1; Galatians 5:13; 2 Corinthians 3:17; 1 Peter 2:16)

---

[1]How did I grow at CGM, and what did I do?
[2]How did CGM make me better? How did God change me? How did the Lord show me himself through others?
Black men/ the ways of Children pointed me to my relationship with the Lord.

Made in the USA
Lexington, KY
21 December 2019